Foundations for Life

A Parent's Guide to Early Childhood Education Approaches

By Ariston Kace

© 2025 Ariston Kace. All rights reserved.

ISBN: 978-1-7643316-1-6

Published by Ariston Kace

Melbourne, Victoria, Australia

This book is a work of nonfiction. Names, environments, and examples are drawn from real-life educational practice and family experience. Any resemblance to actual persons or events is intentional and respectfully portrayed.

© 2025 Ariston Kace

All rights reserved. No part of this publication may be reproduced, stored in a retrieval system, or transmitted in any form or by any means—electronic, mechanical, photocopying, recording, or otherwise—without the prior written permission of the author.

This book is intended for informational and educational purposes only. The author and publisher disclaim any liability arising directly or indirectly from the use of the information contained herein.

To my three children

You are my inspiration, my teachers, and my daily reminder of why this work matters.

Your questions, your laughter, and your unique ways of seeing the world have shaped every page of this guide.

May you always learn with joy, grow with courage, and know how deeply you are loved.

And to every parent walking this path,

This book is for you.

— Ariston Kace

Foreword

As a parent and teacher, I've spent years listening to families ask the same question: "How do I choose the right early childhood setting for my child?" The answer is rarely simple, but it's always personal.

This guide was born from those conversations. It's for the parent standing in a childcare foyer, wondering what questions to ask. It's for the grandparent curious about how things have changed. It's for the educator seeking to explain their philosophy with clarity and heart.

Each chapter reflects not just research and pedagogy, but lived experience. I've seen children thrive in Montessori classrooms, blossom in bush kinder, and find their voice through Reggio-inspired inquiry. I've also seen families struggle to navigate jargon, judgment, and uncertainty.

This book is here to empower you. It's not about choosing the "best" approach; it's about choosing what's best for your child, your family, and your values. I hope it brings clarity, confidence, and connection to your journey.

With warmth and respect,

Ariston Kace

Introduction

Early childhood is a time of wonder, growth, and possibility. It's also a time of big decisions, especially when it comes to choosing an educational approach. With numerous philosophies available, parents often feel overwhelmed, unsure, or pressured to make a quick decision. Sometimes, there are limited options when it comes to availability, but a desire to know how your child will be supported and nurtured in the learning environment is a priority.

Inside, you'll find clear, accessible explanations of 22 early childhood education approaches from Montessori to nature pedagogy, from play-based learning to cultural competence.

Whether you're exploring childcare options, planning your child's transition to school, or simply curious about how children learn, this guide offers clarity and depth. It's designed to be read cover-to-cover or dipped into as needed.

Above all, it's written with respect for children, for families, and for the diverse ways we grow.

Table of Contents

Part 1: Foundations and Philosophies

Exploring the roots of early childhood education through time-tested philosophies that shaped the field.

1. Montessori – Independence Through Discovery 6
2. Reggio Emilia – Learning Through Expression 13
3. Steiner (Waldorf) – Nurturing Imagination 20
4. Froebel – The Power of Play 27
5. Emmi Pikler – Respectful Care and Movement 33
6. HEI Schools (Finnish Model) – Balanced and Playful 40

Part 2: Learning Through Practice

How children learn through structured and emergent teaching strategies, curriculum design, and educator intention.

7. Play-Based Learning – Joyful Exploration 48
8. Inquiry-Based Learning – Asking Big Questions 55
9. Project-Based Learning – Deep Dives into Big Ideas 61
10. Direct Instruction – Structured Skill Building 67
11. Explicit Instruction – Step-by-Step Learning 73
12. Intentional Teaching – Purposeful Moments of Learning 79

13. Event-Based Learning – Shared Experiences............................ 84
14. Emergent Curriculum – Following the Child's Lead 89

Part 3: Whole Child, Whole Community

Approaches that nurture emotional wellbeing, cultural identity, and holistic development—connecting learning to life.

15. Holistic Approach – Whole Child Development 97
16. Cultural Competence – Learning Through Identity 101
17. Respectful Approach – Empathy and Autonomy 105
18. Curiosity Approach – Awe and Wonder 109
19. Attachment-Based Approach – Relationships First................. 113
20. Nature Pedagogy – Learning Through the Land 117
21. Play Schema Theory – Understanding Patterns in Play 121
22. Integrated Approaches – Blending Philosophies...................... 127
23. Eclectic Approach – Responsive and Adaptive Practice 131
24. Choosing What's Right for Your Family 135
25. Foundations for Life 142

Part 1

Foundations and Philosophies

Exploring the roots of early childhood education through time-tested philosophies that shaped the field. These approaches offer deep insight into how children learn, grow, and thrive when given space, respect, and purpose.

In this section, you'll meet foundational thinkers and models that continue to influence classrooms and homes worldwide. From Montessori's independence to Reggio Emilia's creativity, each chapter invites you to discover how philosophy becomes practice and how it might resonate with your child.

Chapter 1: Montessori

Independence Through Discovery

The Montessori approach, developed by Dr Maria Montessori in the early 1900s, is one of the most widely recognised early childhood philosophies in the world. It emphasises independence, self-directed learning, and respect for the child's natural development.

Montessori environments are carefully prepared to support exploration, concentration, and choice. Children are trusted to follow their interests, engage deeply with materials, and develop autonomy through meaningful work.

The Montessori Environment

A Montessori learning environment is a calm, purposeful space designed to honour the child's independence, concentration, and natural desire to learn. It feels more like a thoughtfully arranged home than a traditional room. It is quiet, orderly, and deeply respectful of the child's rhythm.

Upon entering, you'll notice the room is divided into distinct areas: practical life, sensorial, language, mathematics, and cultural studies. Each area contains carefully curated materials displayed on low, open shelves. These materials are not toys; they are considered tools for learning, each with a specific purpose and built-in error control, allowing children to self-correct without adult intervention. Everything is child-sized, from the furniture to the utensils, reinforcing the message: "This space belongs to you."

The practical life area may include trays for tasks such as pouring water, polishing silver, or buttoning fabric squares. These activities build fine motor skills, concentration, and self-confidence. Children move slowly and deliberately, often repeating tasks to master them. You'll see a child sweeping the floor with a miniature broom, another arranging flowers in a vase, and another carefully folding cloth napkins. This is considered meaningful work, as it builds skills and confidence that help children feel capable and valued.

A Montessori-inspired space

In the sensorial area, materials are designed to refine the senses. There are coloured towers, knobbed cylinders, colour tablets and sound boxes. Children explore concepts like size, shape, texture, and sound through hands-on manipulation. The materials are beautiful, being made of wood, glass, and metal, while being arranged with intention. Each item has a designated place and a specific teaching order.

The language area includes sandpaper letters, movable alphabets, and objects for sound matching. Children trace letters with their fingers, build words, and engage in storytelling. The math area features golden beads, number rods, and counting trays that make abstract concepts concrete. Children learn addition, subtraction, and even multiplication through tactile exploration.

Cultural studies introduce geography, botany, zoology, and art. You might see a child working with puzzle maps, classifying leaves, or learning about continents through hands-on activities. There's often a globe, a timeline, and real artifacts that connect children to the broader world.

The environment is quiet but active. Children move freely, choosing their work and engaging deeply with it. There's no loud instruction or chaotic transitions. Instead, educators guide gently, offering lessons when a child is ready and stepping back to allow independent practice. Mixed-age groups foster mentorship and collaboration, with older children helping younger ones.

Natural light, neutral colours, and minimal distractions create a peaceful atmosphere. Plants, artwork, and real-life objects add warmth and beauty. Everything is intentional, from the layout to the language used and is designed to support the child's development and dignity.

In a Montessori classroom, learning is invited. The environment itself is a teacher, offering opportunities for growth, mastery, and joy. Children are trusted to choose, to concentrate, and to care for their space and each other. It's a place where independence flourishes, curiosity is honoured, and every child is seen as capable of constructing their own understanding of the world.

The Role of the Educator

Montessori educators are guides, not instructors. They observe closely, introduce materials at the right moment, and step back to allow the child to lead.

Key educator practices include:

- Preparing the environment with purposeful materials
- Modelling calm, respectful behaviour
- Offering lessons individually or in small groups
- Trusting the child's inner drive to learn
- Supporting independence and self-regulation

Developmental Domains

Cognitive Development

Children engage with hands-on materials that isolate concepts such as size, shape, quantity, and sequence. Learning is concrete, purposeful, and self-paced.

Language and Communication

Montessori supports rich vocabulary development through storytelling, classification, and conversation. Children learn to express themselves clearly and respectfully.

Social and Emotional Development

Mixed-age classrooms foster empathy, leadership, and collaboration. Children learn grace and courtesy, conflict resolution, and emotional regulation.

Physical Development

Fine motor skills are developed through practical life activities, such as pouring, sweeping, buttoning, and other similar tasks. Gross motor development is supported through movement and outdoor play.

Creative and Aesthetic Development

Art, music, and cultural materials are offered with freedom and respect. Creativity is seen as a natural extension of exploration.

Case Study: Leo and the Pouring Work

Leo, age 3, was drawn to a tray with two small pitchers and coloured water. His educator showed him how to pour carefully from one container to another. Leo practised for weeks, self-selecting and engaging with activities that resulted in skill development, such as refining his grip, controlling his movements, and eventually helping younger peers. This simple activity supported Leo's concentration, coordination, and confidence. It also gave him a sense of pride and purpose.

Montessori at Home

You can bring Montessori principles into your home by:

- Creating child-accessible spaces (low shelves, reachable tools)
- Offering real tasks (watering plants, setting the table)
- Encouraging independence in dressing, eating, and cleaning
- Using calm, respectful language
- Observing your child's interests and following their lead

What to Look for in a Montessori Program

Ask yourself:

- Is the environment calm, orderly, and child-sized?
- Are materials purposeful, hands-on, and self-correcting?
- Do educators guide rather than direct?
- Is independence supported across routines and learning?

Ask educators:

- "How do you support self-directed learning?"
- "How do you observe and respond to each child's development?"
- "How do you foster emotional regulation and social skills?"

Parent Pause

Reflect on:

- What tasks could your child take ownership of at home?
- How does your child respond to choice and independence?
- What environments help your child feel calm, focused, and capable?

Montessori is a mindset. It trusts the child's inner drive, respects their pace, and prepares them for lifelong learning. For families seeking calm, purposeful, and independence-building environments, Montessori offers a robust foundation.

Chapter 2: Reggio Emilia

Learning Through Expression

The Reggio Emilia approach originated in post-World War II Italy, founded by educator Loris Malaguzzi and the parents of the town of Reggio Emilia. It is rooted in the belief that children are capable, curious, and full of potential and that learning happens best through relationships, exploration, and expression.

Reggio-inspired environments are rich with materials, documentation, and opportunities for collaboration. Children are seen as protagonists in their own learning, and creativity is at the heart of every experience.

The Reggio Emilia Environment

A Reggio Emilia learning environment is a living, breathing invitation to wonder. It feels less like a classroom and more like a thoughtfully curated studio where every corner whispers possibility and every material holds the potential for storytelling, experimentation, and connection.

Natural light floods the space, often through large windows that frame views of trees, gardens, or shared outdoor areas. The walls are soft and neutral, allowing the colours of children's work to shine. Instead of commercial posters or plastic toys, you'll find open-ended materials such as clay, wire, fabric, wood, and glass beads arranged in baskets, trays, and jars at child height. These materials are considered tools for thinking, expressing, and collaborating.

The room is divided into zones, each with a distinct purpose but fluid boundaries. There might be an atelier or studio space where children explore the visual arts with fundamental tools, including brushes, inks, recycled objects, and provocations such as mirrors or light tables. Nearby, a construction area offers blocks, ramps, and loose parts for building and engineering. A dramatic play corner might include real kitchen tools, dress-up clothes, and miniature furniture, encouraging role-play rooted in real-world experiences.

Documentation is everywhere. Photographs of children in action, transcripts of their conversations, and samples of their work are displayed at eye level, not as decoration, but as evidence of learning. These displays are dynamic, evolving in response to the children's inquiries. They show that the environment is listening to the child, responding to their ideas, and honouring their voice.

Furniture is child-sized and movable. Tables are arranged to support small group collaboration. You will not see rows of individual desks. Shelves are open and accessible, inviting children to choose, combine, and return materials independently. Plants, stones, shells, and other natural elements are woven throughout the space, reinforcing a connection to the earth and a sense of calm.

The environment extends outdoors. A Reggio-inspired outdoor space might include mud kitchens, garden beds, climbing structures made from natural materials, and open-ended tools for water play, sand exploration, and movement. Children move freely between indoors and outdoors, often bringing ideas from one space to the other.

Sound is considered too. The space is designed to support conversation, not noise. Soft rugs, textiles, and acoustic panels help create a gentle hum of activity. Educators speak with intention, listening more than they direct, and children's voices are treated as central to the learning process.

Above all, a Reggio Emilia environment is relational, with it being considered as a co-teacher. It reflects the values of respect, curiosity, and collaboration. It adapts to the children's interests, evolves with their projects, and invites families to participate in the journey. It's a space where learning is visible, creativity is honoured, and every child is seen as capable of constructing knowledge through exploration and expression.

A Reggio Emilia-Inspired Space

In this environment, children don't just learn, they belong. They co-create meaning with peers, educators, and the world around them. And that sense of belonging is the heartbeat of Reggio Emilia.

The Role of the Educator

Educators in Reggio Emilia settings are co-learners, researchers, and documenters. They listen deeply, provoke inquiry, and reflect alongside children.

Key educator practices include:

- Designing environments that invite exploration
- Documenting learning through photos, transcripts, and displays
- Encouraging collaboration and dialogue
- Supporting long-term projects based on children's interests
- Valuing multiple forms of expression ("the hundred languages of children")

The Hundred Languages of Children

In the Reggio Emilia approach, children are seen as rich in potential with a hundred ways to express themselves, not just one. This idea, often referred to as the "hundred languages of children," invites us to recognise that children communicate through a range of means, including drawing, building, movement, dramatic play, music, conversation, and more. Each "language" is a valid and powerful tool for thinking, exploring, and sharing ideas. As parents, when we listen beyond words, when we notice the story in a child's painting, the theory in their block tower, or the emotion in their dance, we begin to understand their inner world. Reggio reminds us that learning is not linear, and expression is not limited to speech. By being aware and honouring all the ways our children communicate, we nurture their creativity, confidence, and connection to the world around them.

Developmental Domains

Cognitive Development

Children engage in complex thinking through projects, problem-solving, and group inquiry. Learning is emergent, contextual, and deeply connected to real-world ideas.

Language and Communication

Dialogue is central. Children express their ideas through conversation, storytelling, drawing, sculpture, and other forms of expression. Educators transcribe and revisit children's words to deepen understanding.

Social and Emotional Development

Group work fosters empathy, negotiation, and shared meaning-making. Children learn to listen, compromise, and build community.

Physical Development

Fine motor skills are developed through activities such as art, construction, and the use of tools. Gross motor development is supported through movement, outdoor play, and spatial exploration.

Creative and Aesthetic Development

Art is valued as a process of thinking. Children use a variety of materials to express their ideas, emotions, and theories. Beauty and intentionality are woven into the environment.

Case Study: Maya and the Shadow Project

Maya, age 4, noticed her shadow stretching across the playground. Her curiosity sparked a group investigation: What makes shadows? Can we change them? Children explored with flashlights, traced outlines, and built shadow sculptures. Educators documented their theories and created a display that evolved over weeks.

This project supported scientific thinking, collaboration, and expressive language, all of which are rooted in Maya's moment of wonder.

Reggio Emilia at Home

You can bring Reggio principles into your home by:

- Creating an "atelier" space with open-ended art materials
- Displaying your child's work and words with respect
- Asking open-ended questions ("What do you think will happen?")
- Documenting learning moments through photos and notes
- Following your child's interests into mini-projects

What to Look for in a Reggio-Inspired Program

Ask yourself:

- Is the environment rich with materials and documentation?

- Are children's ideas visible and valued?
- Do educators listen and respond with curiosity?

Ask educators:

- "How do you support long-term inquiry?"
- "How do you document and revisit children's learning?"
- "How do you encourage collaboration and creativity?"

Parent Pause

Reflect on:

- What does your child express through art, movement, or storytelling?
- How do you respond to their questions and theories?
- What materials or spaces spark their curiosity?

Reggio Emilia honours the child as a thinker, artist, and collaborator. It invites families to see learning as a shared journey that unfolds through dialogue, creativity, and deep respect. For families who value expression, community, and emergent learning, Reggio offers a vibrant path forward.

Chapter 3: Steiner (Waldorf)

Nurturing Imagination

The Steiner approach, also known as Waldorf education, was founded by Austrian philosopher Rudolf Steiner in the early 20th century. It emphasises imagination, rhythm, and holistic development, in turn nurturing the head, heart, and hands of every child.

Steiner environments are warm, artistic, and deeply connected to the natural world. Learning unfolds through storytelling, movement, and creative expression, with a strong focus on emotional wellbeing and developmental readiness.

The Steiner Environment

A Steiner (Waldorf) learning environment feels like stepping into a storybook. It is gentle, rhythmic, and deeply human with a space designed not just for learning, but for living. Every detail, from the colour of the walls to the texture of the materials, is chosen to nurture the child's imagination, emotional wellbeing, and sense of belonging.

The room is warm and inviting, often painted in soft, earthy tones like peach, rose, or golden yellow. Natural light filters through sheer curtains, casting a gentle glow across wooden floors and handmade furnishings. There's a sense of calm and spaciousness without harsh lighting, no clutter and no overstimulation. Instead, the environment breathes with the rhythm of the day.

Furniture is child-sized and made from natural materials, including wooden tables, woven baskets, and wool rugs. Shelves hold carefully selected toys and tools, including hand-carved animals, knitted dolls, silk scarves, and beeswax crayons. These materials are open-ended and beautiful, inviting children to create, imagine, and care for their space. Plastic is rarely found here; instead, the emphasis is on the sensory richness of wood, wool, cotton, and stone.

The day unfolds in a predictable rhythm, which is reflected in the environment itself. There's a space for circle time, where children gather to sing seasonal songs, recite verses, and move together in choreographed gestures. A storytelling corner might feature a simple puppet stage, a basket of props, and a felted backdrop. Stories are told from memory, often repeated over days or weeks, allowing children to internalise language, imagery, and meaning.

Art is central, offering numerous opportunities and resources to support artistic expression. An easel stands ready with watercolour paints in soft hues such as rose, blue, and gold after being mixed by the teacher and offered with reverence. Children paint slowly, often to music, exploring colour and mood rather than technique. Nearby, a handwork table offers knitting needles, felting wool, and embroidery hoops. These activities build fine motor skills, patience, and a sense of accomplishment.

The outdoor space is an extension of the classroom. It might include a garden, mud kitchen, climbing logs, and a sandpit shaded by trees. Children spend a generous amount of time outside, exploring the seasons, caring for plants, and engaging in imaginative play. Nature is often regarded as a teacher and a source of wonder.

There's a quiet hum to the Steiner environment. Children speak softly, move intentionally, and engage deeply. Educators model grace and presence, guiding through imitation rather than instruction. Transitions are gentle, being marked by song, gesture, or ritual. Even cleanup is a shared, meaningful task.

Seasonal changes are celebrated through decorations, stories, and festivals. Autumn might bring lantern walks and apple baking; spring might invite flower crowns and garden planting. These rhythms connect children to the natural cycles and the passage of time.

Above all, a Steiner learning environment is soulful. It honours childhood as a sacred time, protects the imagination, and fosters a deep sense of beauty, connection, and inner life. It's a place where children don't just learn, they grow, dream, and become.

The Role of the Educator

Steiner educators are storytellers, artists, and guides. They create rhythm and ritual, model reverence, and foster a sense of wonder.

Key educator practices include:

- Leading with imagination and narrative
- Creating predictable daily and seasonal rhythms
- Integrating movement, music, and art into every lesson
- Delaying formal academics until developmental readiness
- Supporting emotional and spiritual growth

Developmental Domains

Cognitive Development

Learning is experiential and imaginative. Early years focus on play and storytelling, with formal academics introduced gradually through artistic and rhythmic methods.

Language and Communication

Rich oral language is central. Educators tell stories, sing songs, and recite verses. Children develop vocabulary, listening skills, and expressive language through repetition and rhythm.

Social and Emotional Development

Steiner classrooms emphasise harmony, empathy, and inner life. Children learn through imitation, shared rituals, and consistent relationships with educators and peers.

Physical Development

Movement is woven into the day, being visible during circle time, outdoor play, and purposeful activities such as baking or crafts. Fine motor skills are developed through activities such as knitting, drawing, and sculpting.

Creative and Aesthetic Development

Art is everywhere. Children paint with watercolours, model beeswax, and engage in seasonal crafts. The environment itself is beautiful, consisting of soft colours, natural materials, and handmade objects.

Case Study: Luca and the Puppet Story

Luca, age 5, was captivated by a puppet story about a forest gnome and a lost star. He retold the tale for days, using scarves and pinecones to recreate scenes. His educator noticed Luca's interest and invited the class to create their own puppet show. Through this, Luca practised sequencing, expressive language, and collaboration. All of which were sparked by a moment of imaginative engagement.

Steiner Inspiration for Home

You can bring Steiner principles into your home by:

- Creating gentle rhythms for meals, play, and rest
- Telling stories and singing songs daily
- Using natural materials for play and art
- Celebrating seasonal changes with rituals and crafts
- Limiting screen time to protect imagination

What to Look for in a Steiner Program

Ask yourself:

- Is the environment calm, natural, and handmade?
- Are stories, movement, and art central to the day?
- Is emotional wellbeing prioritised?

Ask educators:

- "How do you support imagination and inner development?"
- "How do you introduce academics in a Steiner-aligned way?"
- "How do you create rhythm and ritual in the classroom?"

Parent Pause

Reflect on:

- What rhythms help your child feel secure and calm?

- How does your child express imagination through play?
- What stories or songs resonate most in your home?

Steiner education nurtures the whole child, their body, mind, and spirit. It invites families to slow down, honour childhood, and embrace the magic of imagination. For families seeking warmth, rhythm, and creative depth, Steiner offers a gentle and soulful path.

Chapter 4: Froebel

The Power of Play

The Froebel-inspired approach, developed by Friedrich Fröbel in the 19th century, is considered the foundation of modern early childhood education. Froebel coined the term "kindergarten," meaning "children's garden," and believed that play is the highest expression of human development in early childhood.

This approach emphasises creativity, hands-on exploration, and the interconnectedness of all things. Froebel saw children as naturally curious and capable, and he designed environments and materials to support their holistic growth intellectually, emotionally, physically, and spiritually.

The Froebel-Inspired Environment

A Froebel-inspired learning environment feels like a garden of ideas that are calm, intentional, and alive with possibility. It's a space where play is not just permitted but revered, and where every material invites exploration, creativity, and connection.

The room is warm and orderly, with natural light streaming across wooden floors and soft rugs. Shelves display Froebel's "gifts", which look like beautifully crafted geometric shapes made of wood, paper, and fabric. These include spheres, cubes, cylinders, sticks, rings, and folding papers, each designed to help children explore forms and patterns.

Materials are arranged with care, inviting children to choose, combine, and design.

There's a sense of rhythm and flow. The day begins with songs and finger rhymes, followed by free play, outdoor time, and creative projects. Educators guide gently, observing children's interests and offering provocations that deepen their thinking. You might see a child building a tower with blocks, another drawing spirals with coloured pencils, and a group crafting flower crowns from garden clippings.

Nature is central. The outdoor space includes garden beds, climbing logs, and quiet corners for reflection. Children dig, plant, observe insects, and collect leaves, learning through direct engagement with the living world. Indoors, natural materials like pinecones, shells, and stones are used for sorting, patterning, and storytelling.

Art and music are woven into the environment. Watercolour paintings hang beside woven tapestries and clay sculptures. A corner might hold rhythm instruments such as tambourines, bells, and wooden drums for spontaneous music-making. Children sing throughout the day, using melody to mark transitions and express emotion.

Furniture is child-sized and movable. Tables support small group collaboration, while floor cushions invite quiet play. The space is uncluttered yet rich, with each item carefully chosen for its beauty, purpose, and potential. There's no overstimulation, only a gentle invitation.

Documentation is subtle. Educators record children's play through notes, photos, observations and learning stories, using them to reflect and plan. Displays show children's work with respect, often accompanied by their captured words or questions.

Above all, the Froebel environment is relational. It supports connection to self, to others, to nature and to ideas. It's a place where children feel safe to explore, express, and grow. Learning is not rushed; it's nurtured, like a seed in fertile soil.

The Role of the Educator

Froebel educators are facilitators of play and discovery. They observe closely, provide meaningful materials, and guide children toward deeper understanding through conversation and reflection.

Key educator practices include:

- Offering symbolic and open-ended materials
- Encouraging self-expression through play and art
- Supporting connections between nature, self, and community
- Creating a balance of freedom and structure
- Valuing each child's unique developmental path

Developmental Domains

Cognitive Development

Children explore patterns, relationships, and problem-solving through Froebel's "gifts" and "occupations" by utilising hands-on materials that support mathematical and spatial thinking.

Language and Communication

Play and storytelling foster rich language development. Educators engage in meaningful dialogue, encouraging children to describe, narrate, and reflect.

Social and Emotional Development

Group play builds empathy, cooperation, and emotional resilience. Children learn to share, negotiate, and express feelings through symbolic play.

Physical Development

Fine motor skills are developed through activities such as building, folding, drawing, and crafting. Gross motor play is supported through movement games and outdoor exploration.

Creative and Aesthetic Development

Art, music, and nature are central to the experience. Children express themselves through drawing, singing, and creating with natural and crafted materials.

Case Study: Scarlett and the Pattern Blocks

Scarlett, age 4, spent days arranging wooden blocks into intricate mandalas. Her educator noticed her fascination with symmetry and encouraged her to explore folding paper shapes and drawing spirals. Scarlett's play evolved into a collaborative mural with her peers, blending math, art, and storytelling.

Froebel-Inspired Ideas at Home

You can bring Froebel principles into your home by:

- Offering natural and geometric materials for play
- Encouraging outdoor exploration and gardening
- Creating time for uninterrupted imaginative play
- Using songs, finger rhymes, and movement games
- Supporting your child's creative projects with patience and interest

What to Look for in a Froebel-Inspired Program

Ask yourself:

- Is play central and deeply respected?
- Are materials open-ended and symbolic?
- Is nature integrated into daily learning?

Ask educators:

- "How do you use Froebel's gifts and occupations?"
- "How do you support creativity and connection?"
- "How do you balance freedom and structure?"

Parent Pause

Reflect on:

- What materials spark your child's creativity?
- How does your child use play to express ideas or emotions?
- What outdoor spaces support your child's sense of wonder?

Froebel's vision of early childhood education was revolutionary in its simplicity: that play is not a distraction from learning, but its deepest form. In a Froebel-inspired environment, children are given the time, space, and materials to explore their inner worlds and the world around them. They build, imagine, and connect, resulting in the development of not just skills, but a sense of self and belonging.

This approach reminds us that education is not just about outcomes. It invites families to see play as purposeful, creativity as essential, and nature as a co-teacher. For those seeking a gentle, holistic, and profoundly respectful path, Froebel offers a timeless foundation.

Chapter 5: Emmi Pikler

Respectful Care and Movement

The Emmi Pikler approach centres on respectful caregiving, free movement, and trust in the child's natural development. Developed by Hungarian paediatrician Emmi Pikler in the mid-20th century, this philosophy emphasises the importance of secure relationships, uninterrupted play, and bodily autonomy, especially in infancy and toddlerhood.

Pikler's work is often associated with the RIE (Resources for Infant Educarers) movement, and her influence can be seen in infant care programs worldwide. At its core, this approach encourages adults to slow down, observe, and respond with empathy, laying a foundation of trust and confidence from the outset.

A Pikler Learning Environment

A Pikler-inspired learning environment is serene, spacious, and deeply respectful of the child's autonomy. It's designed to support free movement, secure relationships, and uninterrupted play, especially for infants and toddlers. The atmosphere is calm and unhurried, with every detail chosen to honour the child's developmental rhythm.

The space is open and uncluttered, with soft lighting and neutral tones, and there are no bright posters or overstimulating toys. Instead, there are simple, natural materials arranged with intention. Low shelves hold baskets of wooden blocks, cloths, and everyday objects that invite exploration. The floor is padded or carpeted, allowing children to roll, crawl, and climb safely.

Furniture is minimal and child-sized. Instead of high chairs or swings, you'll find low tables for shared meals and climbing frames that children can access independently. Pikler environments avoid placing children in positions they cannot reach on their own, so you won't see infants propped up or walkers in use. Movement is trusted, not managed.

Caregiving spaces are central. Nappy changes, feeding, and dressing happen slowly, with full attention and verbal connection. Educators speak gently, narrating each step and waiting for the child's response. These routines are not rushed; they are moments of relationship-building and emotional attunement.

You might see a baby lying on their back, gazing at their hands, or reaching for a nearby toy. No one interrupts. The educator observes quietly, trusting the child's process. Toddlers climb, balance, and explore with confidence, knowing they are safe and supported.

The outdoor area is equally intentional. It may include grassy slopes, low platforms, and natural textures for sensory exploration. Children move freely between indoors and outdoors, choosing their own pace and path.

The sound is soft, with no background music or loud instructions. Instead, you'll hear the gentle rhythm of caregiving, the quiet hum of play, and the occasional joyful squeal of discovery. Educators speak with warmth and clarity, always addressing the child directly and respectfully.

An Emmi Pikler-inspired space.

Documentation is subtle. Educators take notes, photos, and observations to understand each child's development, but displays are minimal. The focus is on presence, not performance.

Above all, a Pikler environment is built on trust. It trusts the child to move, explore, express, and grow. It trusts the adult to observe, to respond, and to build secure relationships. It's a space where autonomy is nurtured from birth, and where every moment, no matter how small, is treated with dignity and care.

The Role of the Educator

Pikler educators are attuned, patient, and deeply respectful. They build secure relationships through consistent, predictable care, allowing children to move, explore, and play without interference.

Key educator practices include:

- Speaking slowly and respectfully during caregiving routines
- Allowing children to initiate movement and play
- Observing without interrupting
- Creating safe, open environments for free movement
- Supporting emotional security through consistent relationships

Developmental Domains

Cognitive Development

Children learn through self-initiated exploration. Problem-solving, spatial awareness, and cause-and-effect understanding emerge naturally through movement and play

Language and Communication

Language is modelled through calm, respectful dialogue during caregiving moments. Educators narrate actions and listen attentively, fostering trust and expressive language.

Social and Emotional Development

Secure attachment is foundational. Children develop confidence, autonomy, and emotional regulation through consistent, attuned relationships.

Physical Development

Gross motor development is prioritised. Children are never placed in positions they cannot reach independently. Movement unfolds naturally with rolling, crawling, sitting, and standing occurring without adult manipulation.

Creative and Aesthetic Development

Creativity emerges through open-ended play with simple, natural materials. Children explore textures, shapes, and movement freely.

Case Study: Theo and the Climbing Frame

Theo, age 1, spent weeks pulling himself up on a low climbing frame. His educator never placed him on top or rushed his progress. One day, Theo climbed to the second rung, paused, and smiled. He had mastered the movement on his own terms. This moment reflected not just physical growth, but confidence, autonomy, and joy.

Emmi Pikler Inspiration for the Home

You can bring Pikler principles into your home by:

- Slowing down during processes such as nappy changes, feeding and dressing
- Speaking respectfully and narrating caregiving routines
- Creating safe spaces for free movement
- Avoiding placing children in positions they cannot reach independently
- Observing play without interrupting

What to Look for in a Pikler-Inspired Program

Ask yourself:

- Are caregiving routines calm, respectful, and unrushed?
- Is movement self-initiated and uninterrupted?
- Are relationships consistent and emotionally attuned?

Ask educators:

- "How do you support secure attachment?"
- "How do you approach infant movement and autonomy?"
- "How do you observe and respond to each child's cues?"

Parent Pause

Reflect on:

- How do you approach caregiving moments with your child?
- What movements has your child mastered independently?
- How do you support autonomy and emotional security?

An Emmi Pikler-inspired learning environment is a sanctuary of respectful simplicity, where infants and toddlers are invited to move, explore, and engage at their own pace. By slowing down, observing, and trusting the child's natural development, we create environments that foster autonomy, confidence, and emotional security. For families seeking a respectful and attachment-based beginning, Pikler offers a gentle yet powerful foundation.

Chapter 6: HEI Schools (Finnish Model)

Balanced and Playful

The HEI Schools model is a contemporary Finnish approach to early childhood education, developed in collaboration with the University of Helsinki. It blends academic research with playful learning, emphasising wellbeing, creativity, and equity. Rooted in Finland's globally respected education system, HEI Schools prioritise joy, autonomy, and holistic development.

This approach is designed to be adaptable across cultures, offering a flexible framework that supports children's natural curiosity while ensuring high-quality pedagogy. It's a model that trusts educators, values play, and sees every child as competent and capable.

A HEI Schools Environment

A HEI Schools learning environment is bright, open, and infused with joy. It's designed to support autonomy, creativity, and emotional wellbeing, blending the best of Finnish pedagogy with playful, child-centred design. The atmosphere is calm but lively, with spaces that invite movement, collaboration, and curiosity.

Natural light fills the room, bouncing off pale wood floors and soft textiles. The colour palette is gentle, featuring muted blues, greens, and yellows that create a sense of calm and focus. Furniture is modular and child-sized, allowing children to rearrange tables, cushions, and play structures to suit their needs. There's no rigid layout; instead, there are flexible zones that adapt to the flow of the day.

Materials are open-ended and accessible. You'll find art supplies, building blocks, recycled objects, and natural items, such as pinecones and stones. Shelves are low and open, encouraging independence and choice. Children select what they need, combine materials creatively, and return them with care.

The environment supports inquiry. There might be a science corner with magnifying glasses and plants, a design area with cardboard and tape, and a cozy reading nook with multilingual books. Educators set up provocations such as a tray of melting ice or a collection of musical instruments and observe how children respond. Learning emerges from play, not from instruction.

Emotional wellbeing is visible. There's a "feelings wall" where children can place symbols representing their mood, and quiet corners for self-regulation. Educators model empathy, validate emotions, and guide children through conflict with calm, respectful dialogue.

Movement is encouraged. Children climb, balance, dance, and stretch throughout the day. The outdoor space serves as an extension of the classroom, featuring natural terrain, loose parts, and areas for gardening, water play, and exploration. Children move freely between indoors and outdoors, choosing where and how to engage.

Documentation is collaborative. Educators photograph learning moments, transcribe children's words, and display projects with pride. Children help curate their own portfolios, reflecting on what they've learned and what they want to explore next.

HEI Schools inspired learning space

Sound is gentle and purposeful. You'll hear laughter, music, and conversation, but rarely shouting or chaos. Transitions are marked with songs or rituals, and the pace of the day is flexible, allowing children to immerse themselves in play without interruption.

Above all, a HEI School's environment is democratic. It trusts children to lead, values their voices, and creates an environment that allows every child to thrive. It's a place where learning feels joyful, meaningful, and deeply connected to the child's world.

The Role of the Educator

HEI educators are facilitators of exploration and emotional wellbeing. They create inclusive environments, observe, and support children's agency through playful, intentional interactions.

Key educator practices include:

- Planning flexible, child-led activities
- Supporting emotional regulation and social skills
- Encouraging inquiry and experimentation
- Building trusting relationships with children and families
- Using observation and documentation to guide learning

Developmental Domains

Cognitive Development

Children engage in inquiry-based projects, problem-solving games, and creative challenges. Learning is integrated across domains and driven by curiosity.

Language and Communication

Dialogue is encouraged through storytelling, group discussions, and expressive play. Multilingualism is embraced, and children's voices are central.

Social and Emotional Development

Emotional wellbeing is foundational. Educators support self-awareness, empathy, and peer collaboration through daily routines and play.

Physical Development

Movement is embedded throughout the day. Children climb, dance, build, and explore both indoors and outdoors, developing coordination and confidence.

Creative and Aesthetic Development

Art, music, and design are celebrated. Children express themselves through diverse media and are encouraged to explore beauty, pattern, and form.

Case Study: Sari and the Sound Garden

Sari, age 5, was fascinated by the sounds of nature. Her educator helped her and her peers create a "sound garden" using recycled materials, musical instruments, and natural objects. The children explored pitch, rhythm, and vibration, blending science, art, and play. Sari's curiosity led to a week-long project that culminated in a performance for families.

HEI at Home

You can bring HEI principles into your home by:

- Encouraging open-ended play and inquiry
- Supporting emotional expression through conversation and art
- Creating flexible routines that allow for choice and autonomy
- Exploring nature and everyday phenomena together
- Valuing your child's ideas and questions

What to Look For in a HEI-Inspired Program

Ask yourself:

- Is play central to the learning experience?
- Are children's ideas respected and explored?
- Is emotional wellbeing actively supported?

Ask educators:

- "How do you integrate play and inquiry?"
- "How do you support children's emotional development?"
- "How do you adapt learning to each child's interests?"

Parent Pause

Reflect on:

- What questions does your child ask most often?
- How do you support their emotional and creative expression?
- What routines help your child feel balanced and joyful?

The HEI Schools model offers a refreshing blend of research-based pedagogy and playful freedom. It reminds us that children learn best when they feel safe, seen, and inspired. For families seeking balance, creativity, and emotional depth, the Finnish approach offers a joyful and adaptable foundation.

Part 2

Learning Through Practice

How children learn through structured and emergent teaching strategies, curriculum design, and the intention of educators.

In Part 2, we examine how children learn through intentional teaching strategies, effective curriculum design, and responsive educator practices. These approaches range from structured instruction to emergent, child-led inquiry, and each offers unique insights into how learning unfolds in early childhood.

While philosophies like Montessori and Reggio Emilia emphasise the environment and the child's role as protagonist, the approaches in this section focus more closely on the how of learning: how educators plan, observe, and respond; how curriculum is shaped; and how play, inquiry, and instruction intersect.

You'll encounter models that prioritise joy and spontaneity, like play-based and inquiry-based learning, alongside those that offer clarity and structure, such as direct and explicit instruction. You'll also explore hybrid approaches, such as event-based learning and intentional teaching, that bridge child-led exploration with educator guidance.

These chapters invite reflection on your child's learning style, your family's values, and the kind of educational rhythm that feels right.

Whether your child thrives with freedom or flourishes with routine, Part 2 offers tools to help you recognise and support their unique learning journey.

Above all, this section reinforces a core truth: learning is not a one-size-fits-all approach. It's dynamic, relational, and deeply personal. By understanding these varied approaches, you'll be better equipped to choose environments that nurture your child's curiosity, confidence, and growth.

Chapter 7: Play-Based Learning

Joyful Exploration

Play-based learning is one of the most widely adopted approaches in early childhood education in Australia. It recognises play as the natural language of children. A powerful medium through which they explore, express, and understand the world around them. In this model, play is not a break from learning; it is learning.

Educators create environments rich in materials, relationships, and opportunities for imaginative, physical, and social play. Through play, children develop foundational skills across all domains, including problem-solving, communication, creativity, and emotional regulation.

A play-based learning environment is vibrant, flexible, and alive with possibility. It's a space where children's ideas take centre stage, and where every corner invites exploration, creativity, and connection. The atmosphere is joyful and dynamic, with a hum of activity that reflects deep engagement.

The room is divided into zones: dramatic play, construction, art, sensory, reading, and quiet reflection. Each area is stocked with open-ended materials, such as blocks, fabric, puppets, natural items, and recycled objects, that children can use in countless ways. Shelves are low and accessible, encouraging independence and choice. Nothing is fixed, and everything can be rearranged to suit the evolving interests of the children.

In the dramatic play area, you might find a kitchen one day and a spaceship the next. Children dress up, assign roles, and create elaborate narratives. Educators observe and add props to enrich the story. You might see menus, maps, or notebooks provided by educators without children being directed to play. The construction zone is filled with blocks, ramps, and connectors. Children build towers, bridges, and cities, testing ideas and solving problems collaboratively.

The art area offers paints, clay, collage materials, and drawing tools. Children create freely, expressing emotions, ideas, and stories. Their work is displayed with pride, often accompanied by their words. The sensory table may hold water, sand, rice, or mud, inviting tactile exploration and scientific inquiry.

Movement is encouraged. Children dance, climb, balance, and stretch throughout the day. The outdoor space serves as an extension of the classroom, featuring loose parts, natural terrain, and areas for gardening, water play, and imaginative adventures. Children move freely between indoors and outdoors, choosing where and how to engage.

Sound is lively but purposeful with an environment filled with laughter, storytelling, negotiation, and bursts of song. Educators speak with warmth and clarity, joining play when invited and offering gentle scaffolding when needed. Transitions are marked with songs, rituals, or visual cues, thereby maintaining a smooth flow without abrupt interruptions.

Documentation is visible, including photos, transcripts, and artifacts of play, which are displayed at child height, showing that their work is valued and understood. Educators use these records to reflect, plan, and share learning with families.

Above all, a play-based environment is relational. It honours the child's voice, supports emotional expression, and fosters a sense of belonging. It's a place where learning is joyful, spontaneous, and deeply meaningful and where children are free to be themselves, explore their world, and grow through play. Play-based learning is particularly effective for children experiencing disadvantage. It allows for differentiated engagement, cultural responsiveness, and trauma-informed practice.

The Role of the Educator

Play-based educators are facilitators, observers, and co-players. They follow the child's lead, extend ideas, and create conditions for deep engagement.

Key educator practices include:

- Designing open-ended, engaging environments
- Observing play to understand developmental needs
- Joining play respectfully to scaffold learning
- Encouraging collaboration and negotiation
- Valuing play as purposeful and complex

Benefits of Play-Based Learning

Holistic Development

Play supports the whole child in mind, body, and spirit. It integrates physical movement, emotional expression, social interaction, and cognitive exploration. For example, building a fort involves gross motor skills, spatial reasoning, negotiation, and imaginative storytelling.

Agency and Autonomy

In play, children make choices, solve problems, and direct their own learning. This fosters independence, confidence, and a sense of ownership. When educators follow children's lead, they affirm the child's voice and capacity.

Deep Engagement

Play is intrinsically motivating. Children persist longer, explore more deeply, and take greater risks when they are engaged in play. This leads to sustained attention and richer learning outcomes.

Differentiated Learning

Play allows children to engage at their own level. A child exploring trajectory might throw balls, roll cars, or build ramps, each activity reflecting their developmental stage and interest. Educators can observe these schemas and respond with tailored provocations.

Social Learning

Play is a social laboratory where children learn to share, negotiate, empathise, and collaborate. They explore roles, rules, and relationships, developing the skills needed for citizenship and community life.

Creativity and Innovation

Play invites imagination. Children invent worlds, transform materials, and solve problems in novel ways. This creativity is the foundation of innovation and adaptability.

Case Study: Ava and the Vet Clinic

Ava, age 4, transformed the dramatic play corner into a veterinary clinic. She organised tools, assigned roles, and cared for stuffed animals with empathy and precision. Her educator observed and added clipboards, bandages, and books about animals. Over the course of two weeks, Ava's play evolved into a collaborative project that involved math (measuring medicine), literacy (writing pet records), and science (learning about habitats).

Play-based learning at home

You can bring play-based principles into your home by:

- Creating time and space for uninterrupted play
- Offering open-ended materials (blocks, fabric, natural items)
- Joining your child's play with curiosity and respect
- Encouraging storytelling and role-play
- Valuing play as meaningful, not just recreational

What to Look for in a Play-Based Program

Ask yourself:

- Is play central and protected throughout the day?
- Are materials varied, open-ended, and accessible?
- Are children's ideas and stories visible?

Ask educators:

- "How do you observe and extend children's play?"
- "How do you balance free play with intentional teaching?"
- "How do you support social and emotional learning through play?"

Parent Pause

Reflect on:

- What types of play does your child gravitate toward?
- How do you respond when your child invites you into their play?
- What does your child express through imaginative or physical play?

Play-based learning is grounded in the understanding that children make sense of the world through exploration, imagination, and relationships. When thoughtfully supported, play becomes a rich medium for developing cognitive, social, emotional, and physical skills.

Given the time, space, and trust to play, children develop the skills, confidence, and creativity they need for life. For families seeking a nurturing, dynamic, and child-led approach, play-based learning offers a powerful and enduring path.

Chapter 8: Inquiry-Based Learning

Asking Big Questions

Inquiry-Based Learning is a dynamic approach that places children's questions, curiosities, and investigations at the heart of the learning process. Rather than delivering predetermined content, educators guide children in exploring real-world topics through observation, experimentation, and reflection.

This model encourages critical thinking, collaboration, and deep engagement. Children become researchers, posing questions, testing ideas and constructing knowledge through hands-on exploration. Inquiry-based learning fosters a sense of agency and wonder, helping children see themselves as capable learners and thinkers.

An inquiry-based learning environment is a laboratory of curiosity. It is flexible, responsive, and alive with questions. It's designed to support deep thinking, collaborative exploration, and authentic engagement with the world. The atmosphere is calm but intellectually vibrant, with children immersed in meaningful investigations.

The space is organised into zones that invite inquiry: a science corner with magnifying glasses and natural specimens, a construction area with recycled materials and blueprints, and a documentation wall filled with children's questions, drawings, and theories. Materials are open-ended and accessible, allowing children to test ideas, build models, and represent their thinking in diverse ways.

You might see a group of children investigating shadows using flashlights, tracing outlines, and comparing results. Their educator listens, asks probing questions, and documents their discoveries. Nearby, another group explores seeds by planting, measuring, and keeping a journal of their growth. The environment adapts to these inquiries, with new materials and provocations introduced as the investigation deepens. Tables support small group collaboration, while floor cushions and quiet nooks invite reflection. Shelves hold clipboards, cameras, measuring tools, and art supplies, all tools ready and available for inquiry and representation. There's no rigid schedule as the day flows around the children's investigations.

Documentation is central. Educators photograph learning moments, transcribe conversations, and display evolving projects. Children revisit their work, reflect on their thinking, and share insights with peers and families. Learning is visible, celebrated, and an ongoing process.

The outdoor space is equally rich. Children explore natural phenomena by tracking insects, collecting leaves, and building water channels. Educators support inquiry by asking open-ended questions and providing tools for observation and experimentation.

Sound is purposeful where you'll hear children discussing theories, negotiating roles, and expressing excitement. Educators speak with intention, guiding inquiry without dominating it. Transitions are gentle, often marked by reflection.

Above all, an inquiry-based environment values the child's voice, supports collaborative meaning-making, and treats learning as a shared journey. It's a place where questions are honoured, ideas are tested, and knowledge is constructed through experience.

The Role of the Educator

Inquiry-based educators are facilitators, co-investigators, and provocateurs. They listen closely, document learning, and create an environment that fosters discovery.

Key educator practices include:

- Encouraging open-ended questions and dialogue
- Designing provocations that spark curiosity
- Supporting long-term investigations
- Documenting children's thinking and theories
- Valuing process over product

Benefits of Inquiry-Based Learning

Deep Engagement

Inquiry begins with genuine curiosity. When children investigate questions they care about, they become deeply invested in the learning process. This leads to sustained attention, persistence, and a sense of joy.

Critical Thinking

Inquiry teaches children to ask questions, gather information, test ideas, and reflect. These are foundational skills for lifelong learning and citizenship.

Collaboration and Dialogue

Inquiry is often social. Children work together to explore ideas, negotiate meaning, and build shared understanding. This fosters empathy, communication, and teamwork.

Creativity and Innovation

Inquiry invites divergent thinking. Children explore multiple solutions, imagine possibilities, and create new connections. This nurtures creativity and adaptability.

Real-World Relevance

Inquiry connects learning to life. Children investigate topics that matter to them such as topics of interest like weather, insects, or community helpers. Children investigate their interests and apply their findings in meaningful ways.

Educator Responsiveness

Inquiry requires educators to listen, observe, and respond. This builds strong relationships and ensures that learning is tailored to each child's interests and needs.

Case Study: Noah and the Rainwater Question

Noah, age 5, asked, "Where does rain go after it hits the roof?" His educator invited the group to explore. They collected rainwater, built models of gutters, and mapped water flow around the school. Over the course of two weeks, the children tested ideas, interviewed a plumber, and created a documentary. Noah's question became a springboard for science, math, literacy, and community connection.

Inquiry-Based Learning at Home

You can bring inquiry-based principles into your home by:

- Encouraging your child's questions and helping them investigate
- Exploring everyday phenomena together (e.g., cooking, nature walks)
- Creating a "wonder wall" to track curiosities
- Valuing process over quick answers
- Supporting long-term projects based on your child's interests

What to Look for in an Inquiry-Based Program

Ask yourself:

- Are children's questions visible and valued?
- Is learning driven by exploration and investigation?
- Are projects documented and revisited?

Ask educators:

- "How do you support children's inquiries?"
- "How do you balance curriculum goals with emergent learning?"
- "How do you document and reflect on children's thinking?"

Parent Pause

Reflect on:

- What questions does your child ask most often?
- How do you respond when they wonder aloud?
- What tools or spaces support your child's investigations?

Inquiry-based learning empowers children to ask questions, explore, and gain a deeper understanding. It nurtures curiosity, resilience, and a lifelong love of learning. For families seeking depth, flexibility, and authentic engagement, inquiry offers a rich and responsive path.

Chapter 9: Project-Based Learning

Deep Dives into Big Ideas

Project-Based Learning (PBL) is a dynamic approach that centres learning around meaningful, sustained investigations. Children explore real-world topics through hands-on projects that integrate multiple domains, including literacy, numeracy, science, art, and social studies, while developing critical thinking, collaboration, and problem-solving skills.

Rather than isolated lessons, PBL offers immersive experiences. Children pose questions, research answers, create artifacts, and share their findings with others. The process is as important as the product, and learning unfolds through exploration, iteration, and reflection.

Project-based learning is a workshop of ideas. It is flexible, collaborative, and deeply engaging. It's designed to support sustained inquiry, creative expression, and meaningful outcomes. The atmosphere is focused and purposeful, with children immersed in long-term investigations that matter to them.

The space is organised around active work zones: a research area with books, tablets, and writing tools; a design studio with art supplies, blueprints, and recycled materials; and a construction corner with tools, blocks, and building kits. Tables are arranged for collaboration, and shelves hold portfolios, journals, and project artifacts. Children move freely between zones, choosing tools and materials that support their work.

Walls display evolving projects, including photos, sketches, questions, and reflections. You might see a timeline of a community garden, a storyboard for a documentary, or a mural representing a class inquiry into ocean life. These displays are dynamic, showing the learning process as it unfolds.

Educators guide gently. They help children refine questions, locate resources, and reflect on progress. They document learning through notes, transcripts, and visual records, using these to support planning and share growth with families.

The environment supports autonomy. Children choose topics, set goals, and manage their time. They work in small groups, negotiate roles, and offer peer feedback. Educators model collaboration and help resolve challenges with empathy and skill.

The outdoor space is often part of the project. Children might build structures, conduct experiments, or gather data from nature. Movement is purposeful and closely tied to the task at hand.

Sound is productive. You'll hear brainstorming, planning, storytelling, and bursts of excitement. Educators speak with clarity and encouragement, helping children stay focused and inspired.

Technology is used thoughtfully. Children may record interviews, create presentations, or conduct online research. Screens are tools for creation, not passive consumption.

Above all, a project-based environment is empowering. It treats children as capable thinkers, creators, and contributors. It connects learning to life, helping children see their ideas as valuable and their voices as powerful.

The Role of the Educator

Educators in project-based settings are designers, facilitators, and co-learners. They help children identify authentic questions, guide research, and support the creation of meaningful outcomes.

Key educator practices include:

- Designing open-ended, interdisciplinary projects
- Supporting inquiry and sustained engagement
- Encouraging collaboration and peer feedback
- Documenting learning through journals, portfolios, and displays
- Celebrating process, creativity, and growth

Benefits of Project-Based Learning

Integrated Learning

Projects blend multiple domains, including literacy, numeracy, science, and the arts, into a cohesive whole. For example, a garden project might involve measuring soil, writing plant labels, drawing diagrams, and researching pollinators.

Real-World Relevance

Projects connect learning to life. Children investigate topics that matter to them, such as recycling, pets, or community helpers and apply their findings in meaningful ways.

Agency and Ownership

Children co-design projects, make decisions, and reflect on outcomes. This fosters autonomy, confidence, and a sense of pride.

Deep Thinking

Projects require sustained inquiry. Children ask questions, gather information, test ideas, and revise their work. This supports critical thinking and metacognition.

Collaboration and Dialogue

Projects often involve group work. Children learn to listen, compromise, and build shared understanding. This strengthens relationships and social-emotional skills.

Educator Responsiveness

Projects emerge from children's interests. Educators observe, document, and scaffold learning to ensure that each child's voice is heard and valued.

Case Study: Elly and the Butterfly Garden

Elly, age 6, noticed butterflies in the schoolyard and asked, "Can we help them stay?" Her educator supported a class-wide project to create a butterfly garden. Children researched habitats, designed garden layouts, planted native flowers, and created informational signs. The project spanned four weeks and integrated science, math, literacy, and art. Elly's question became a catalyst for community engagement and environmental stewardship.

Project-Based Learning at Home

You can bring project-based principles into your home by:

- Supporting long-term investigations based on your child's interests
- Encouraging planning, research, and creative expression
- Documenting progress through photos, journals, or portfolios
- Celebrating effort and iteration, not just final results
- Sharing projects with family, friends, or community

What to Look for in a Project-Based Curriculum

Ask yourself:

- Are children engaged in sustained, meaningful investigations?
- Is learning interdisciplinary and connected to real life?
- Are children's voices central to project design?

Ask educators:

- "How do you support long-term projects?"
- "How do you integrate curriculum into child-led investigations?"
- "How do you document and share learning outcomes?"

Parent Pause

Reflect on:

- What topics spark your child's curiosity and sustained interest?
- How does your child approach planning and problem-solving?
- What projects could you explore together at home?

Project-Based Learning invites children to dive deep, think big, and create with purpose. It fosters independence, collaboration, and real-world relevance. For families seeking meaningful engagement and interdisciplinary growth, this approach offers a rich and empowering foundation.

Chapter 10: Direct Instruction

Structured Skill Building

In the vibrant hum of early childhood classrooms, learning often unfolds through play, inquiry, and exploration. But there are moments when clarity matters, when a child is learning to form a letter, count to ten, or follow a safety rule. In these moments, Direct instruction offers a structured, intentional approach that supports foundational skill development.

It is a highly structured teaching approach that emphasises clear, explicit instruction, mastery of foundational skills, and systematic progression. Initially developed by Siegfried Engelmann in the 1960s, this model is rooted in the belief that all children can learn when instruction is carefully designed and delivered.

In early childhood settings, Direct Instruction is often used to teach literacy, numeracy, and other core skills through scripted lessons, repetition, and immediate feedback. While it may seem rigid compared to play-based or inquiry-driven models, it offers clarity, consistency, and measurable outcomes, especially for children who benefit from routine and scaffolding.

Shelves hold structured materials, including flashcards, workbooks, manipulatives, and scripted lesson guides. Each item has a designated place, reinforcing order and routine. You'll notice visual cues such as alphabet charts, number lines, behaviour expectations, and step-by-step instructions. These supports help children follow directions, stay on task, and build independence.

Educators lead with clarity. Lessons are broken into small, manageable steps, and children are guided through each one with modelling, repetition, and feedback. For example, a literacy lesson might begin with phonemic awareness, followed by blending sounds, reading words, and practising fluency, all within a tightly structured format.

Children respond chorally, take turns, and receive immediate correction when needed. The pace is brisk but supportive, and educators closely monitor progress. Assessment is ongoing, with data used to inform instruction and groupings.

There's a strong emphasis on mastery. Children practice skills until they reach fluency, and lessons are revisited to reinforce learning. This repetition builds confidence and competence, especially for children who thrive with structure.

Transitions are timed and rehearsed, and physical activities are often linked to academic content, such as clapping syllables or hopping out math problems. Educators use clear, consistent language, and children are taught to listen attentively and respond appropriately. Noise levels are monitored to maintain focus and ensure a smooth workflow.

Above all, direct instruction is intentional. It's built on the belief that children benefit from clarity, consistency, and high expectations. For some learners, especially those who require extra support or benefit from routine, this environment provides a sense of safety and success.

The Role of the Educator

Educators in Direct Instruction settings are instructors, monitors, and motivators. They deliver lessons with precision, track progress, and ensure mastery.

Key educator practices include:

- Using scripted, sequenced lessons
- Modelling skills and guiding practice
- Providing immediate feedback and correction
- Monitoring progress through data and observation
- Reinforcing routines and expectations

Benefits of Direct Instruction

Clarity and Consistency

Direct instruction provides clear explanations, step-by-step guidance, and consistent routines. This helps children understand expectations and reduces confusion.

Efficient Skill Acquisition

Children learn discrete skills, such as letter formation, counting, and following instructions, quickly and accurately. This supports readiness for more complex tasks.

Immediate Feedback

Educators can correct errors, reinforce success, and adjust instruction in real time. This helps children stay on track and feel supported.

Confidence and Independence

When children master foundational skills, they feel capable and confident. This fosters independence and a positive attitude toward learning.

Equity and Inclusion

Direct instruction supports children with diverse learning needs by reducing ambiguity and providing a structured approach to learning. It is especially effective in inclusive classrooms and early intervention programs.

Case Study: Elijah and the Reading Routine

Elijah, age 5, struggled with early literacy. His educator employed a Direct Instruction reading program, incorporating daily phonics practice, guided reading, and fluency drills. Within weeks, Elijah began decoding words independently and gained confidence. The structured routine gave him the clarity and repetition he needed to succeed.

Direct Instruction at Home

You can bring Direct Instruction principles into your home by:

- Practising foundational skills with short, focused sessions
- Using visual cues and step-by-step instructions
- Offering immediate feedback and encouragement
- Creating consistent routines for learning

- Tracking progress and celebrating mastery

What to Look for in a Direct Instruction Program

Ask yourself:

- Is instruction explicit, sequenced, and goal-oriented?
- Are children supported in mastering foundational skills?
- Is progress monitored and shared?

Ask educators:

- "How do you ensure children master key skills?"
- "How do you adapt instruction for different learners?"
- "How do you balance structure with engagement?"

Parent Pause

Reflect on:

- How does your child respond to structure and routine?
- What foundational skills are they currently developing?
- How do you support step-by-step learning at home?

Direct Instruction offers clarity, consistency, and measurable growth. It's especially powerful for children who benefit from routine, repetition, and explicit teaching. For families seeking a structured, skill-focused approach, this model provides a strong and supportive foundation.

Chapter 11: Explicit Instruction

Step-by-Step Learning

Explicit Instruction is a structured teaching approach that emphasises clarity, modelling, and guided practice. It is designed to make learning visible, breaking down complex skills into manageable steps and ensuring children understand what they're learning, why they're learning it, and how to succeed.

This approach is particularly effective for teaching foundational academic skills, including reading, writing, and mathematics. It supports children who benefit from direct guidance, repetition, and scaffolded support, while still allowing room for engagement and success.

An environment rich with explicit instruction is clear, organised, and intentionally designed to support step-by-step learning. It's a space where children know what to expect, where to find materials, and how to engage with tasks confidently.

The room is arranged to support whole-group, small-group, and individual instruction. Tables are set up for focused work, and a central teaching area, often equipped with a whiteboard or interactive display, is used for modelling and demonstration. Visual aids such as anchor charts, word walls, and number lines are displayed prominently, reinforcing key concepts and vocabulary.

Materials are purposeful and accessible. You'll find bins labelled with manipulatives, writing tools, levelled readers, and math games. Each item has a clear use, and children are taught how to use them effectively. There's no clutter, just intentional resources that support the day's learning goals.

Educators lead with clarity. Lessons begin with a clear objective ("Today we're learning to...") followed by modelling ("Watch me as I..."), guided practice ("Let's try it together"), and independent application ("Now you try on your own"). Children receive immediate feedback and are encouraged to ask questions, reflect on their work, and make revisions.

You might see a literacy lesson where the educator models decoding a word, then guides children through blending sounds, followed by individual reading practice. Or a math lesson where children use counters to solve problems, with the educator checking for understanding and adjusting instruction as needed.

The environment supports routine. Children are familiar with the daily routine, the behavioural expectations, and the steps for each task. This predictability builds confidence and reduces anxiety, especially for children who thrive with structure.

Movement is purposeful. Children transition between activities with visual cues or songs. Brain breaks and movement games are used to refresh focus while reinforcing academic content.

Sound is focused. Educators use clear, consistent language, and children are taught to listen actively and respond respectfully. Group discussions are structured, with turn-taking and sentence starters to support the development of expressive language.

Documentation is visible. Children's work is displayed with learning goals attached, showing progress and celebrating effort. Educators use checklists, rubrics, and anecdotal notes to track growth and inform instruction.

Above all, an Explicit Instruction environment is empowering. It helps children understand what success looks like and gives them the tools to achieve it. It's a space where clarity leads to confidence, and where every child is supported in mastering essential skills.

The Role of the Educator

Educators in Explicit Instruction settings are guides, models, and motivators. They break down learning into clear steps and support children through each phase.

Key educator practices include:

- Stating clear learning objectives
- Modelling tasks and strategies
- Providing guided and independent practice
- Giving immediate, constructive feedback
- Monitoring progress and adjusting instruction

Benefits of Explicit Instruction

Clarity and Confidence

Children know what they're learning, why it matters, and how to succeed. This builds confidence and reduces anxiety.

Strategy Development

Children learn how to approach tasks, whether sounding out a word, solving a problem, or managing emotions. These strategies transfer across contexts.

Scaffolding and Support

Educators guide children through new tasks, offering prompts, feedback, and encouragement. This ensures success and builds independence.

Metacognition and Reflection

Children learn to reflect on their own thinking. They reflect on what worked, what didn't, and how to improve. This fosters lifelong learning.

Equity and Accessibility

Explicit instruction makes learning visible and predictable. It supports diverse learners by reducing cognitive load and increasing clarity.

Case Study: Ben and the Writing Ladder

Ben, age 7, struggled with writing complete sentences. His educator introduced a "writing ladder," a visual guide that shows how to build from a word to a sentence to a story. Through modelling, guided practice, and feedback, Ben climbed the ladder over several weeks. He began writing confidently, proud of each step he mastered.

Explicit Instruction at Home

You can bring Explicit Instruction principles into your home by:

- Breaking tasks into clear, manageable steps
- Modelling skills before asking your child to try
- Practising together before independent work
- Using visual aids and checklists to support learning
- Celebrating effort and progress with specific feedback

What do Environments that Support Explicit Teaching Look Like?

Ask yourself:

- Are learning goals clear and visible?
- Is instruction broken into manageable steps?
- Are children supported through modelling and practice?

Ask educators:

- "How do you model and scaffold learning?"
- "How do you track and respond to progress?"
- "How do you support children who need extra guidance?"

Parent Pause

Reflect on:

- What skills is your child currently working to master?

- How do you support learning with clarity and encouragement?
- What routines help your child feel confident and capable?

Explicit Instruction offers clarity, structure, and a path to mastery. It helps children build essential skills with confidence and support. For families seeking a step-by-step, guided approach to learning, this model provides a strong and empowering foundation.

Chapter 12: Intentional Teaching

Purposeful Moments of Learning

Intentional Teaching is a responsive and purposeful approach that blends child-led exploration with educator guidance. It recognises that while children learn through play and inquiry, educators play a vital role in shaping the environment, interactions, and experiences to support developmental goals.

In early childhood education, learning doesn't only happen during planned activities; it occurs in transitions, conversations, and spontaneous discoveries. When a child asks, "Why is the moon out during the day?" or struggles to zip their jacket, the educator's response can either pass the moment by or turn it into a powerful learning opportunity. Intentional teaching is the art of recognising these moments and responding with purpose. It is a pedagogical approach that blends planning with responsiveness, structure with sensitivity.

Educators observe closely, identify teachable moments, and respond with strategies that extend learning. Intentional teaching bridges spontaneity and structure, helping children deepen understanding while honouring their interests and agency.

The educator observes a child building a tower with blocks, then gently asks, "How tall do you think it will be?" This question sparks measurement, prediction, and problem-solving. Nearby, a group is painting. The educator notices their interest in mixing colours and introduces vocabulary like "shade," "hue," and "contrast." These moments are intentional, not scripted, but guided by insight.

Educators are attuned to each child's needs, strengths, and interests, and they use this insight to guide learning in meaningful ways. It's a space where every moment holds potential, and where teaching is a thoughtful act.

The Role of the Educator

Intentional educators are observers, planners, and responsive guides. They strike a balance between spontaneity and purpose, utilising insight to enhance learning.

Key educator practices include:

- Observing play and identifying teachable moments
- Planning flexible experiences that support developmental goals
- Asking open-ended questions to deepen thinking
- Documenting learning and reflecting on practice
- Building strong, respectful relationships with children and families

Benefits of Intentional Teaching

Responsive Learning

Educators respond to children's interests, questions, and needs in real time. This makes learning meaningful, timely, and engaging.

Strong Relationships

Intentional teaching builds trust and connection. Educators listen deeply, respond sensitively, and affirm each child's identity.

Equity and Differentiation

Educators tailor support to each child's strengths, challenges, and context. This ensures that all children can access and succeed in learning.

Integration of Learning

Intentional teaching weaves learning into everyday moments such as mealtimes, play, and transitions. This creates a rich, continuous learning environment.

Professional Reflection

Educators reflect on their practice, plan with purpose, and adapt their approach based on observations. This fosters professional growth and pedagogical clarity.

Case Study: Zara and the Leaf Inquiry

Zara, age 4, collected leaves during outdoor play and asked, "Why are they different shapes?" Her educator documented the question and invited the group to explore. They sorted leaves, made rubbings, researched tree types, and created a leaf museum. The educator guided the inquiry with questions, books, and art, responding to Zara's curiosity with purpose and care.

Intentional Teaching at Home

You can bring Intentional Teaching principles into your home by:

- Observing your child's play and asking thoughtful questions
- Offering materials that support exploration and creativity
- Creating flexible routines that allow for spontaneous learning
- Documenting your child's discoveries through photos or journals
- Responding to interests with books, outings, or projects

What to Look for in an Intentional Teaching Program

Ask yourself:

- Are educators responsive and reflective?
- Is learning guided by observation and insight?
- Are children's interests and strengths honoured?

Ask educators:

- "How do you identify and respond to teachable moments?"
- "How do you plan learning experiences based on observation?"
- "How do you document and share children's learning?"

Parent Pause

Reflect on:

- What interests or questions has your child expressed recently?

- How do you respond to spontaneous learning moments?
- What routines or materials support curiosity at home?

Intentional Teaching combines structure with spontaneity, providing a responsive and respectful approach to learning. It empowers educators to guide with insight and families to support with presence. For those seeking a balanced, thoughtful approach, this model offers depth, flexibility, and connection.

Chapter 13: Event-Based Learning

Learning Through Shared Experiences

Event-based learning is a child-centred approach that uses shared experiences, such as excursions, celebrations, or community projects, as catalysts for learning. It's rooted in the idea that meaningful events spark curiosity, conversation, and collaboration, allowing children to explore concepts across multiple domains in a natural and engaging way.

Rather than following a fixed curriculum, educators plan around real-life happenings and children's responses to them. These events become the foundation for inquiry, storytelling, problem-solving, and creative expression. It's an approach that values relevance, connection, and the richness of lived experience.

Event-Based Learning is dynamic, responsive, and deeply connected to the world beyond the classroom. It's designed to support spontaneous inquiry and collaborative exploration, with space and materials that adapt to the evolving interests of the children.

Events provide rich contexts for vocabulary development, storytelling, and conversation. Studies have found that children exposed to event-based learning demonstrated stronger narrative skills and expressive language.

These events facilitate social and emotional learning, as well as cultural responsiveness. Shared experiences foster empathy, a sense of belonging, and emotional regulation. Event-based learning affirms children's identities by incorporating family traditions, cultural celebrations, and community practices. This supports inclusion, respect, and intercultural understanding.

Events naturally integrate multiple learning areas, including literacy, numeracy, science, and the arts. For example, a cooking event might involve reading recipes, measuring ingredients, exploring chemical changes, and sharing stories.

The Role of the Educator

Educators in Event-Based Learning settings are planners, observers, and co-participants. They use real-life events to spark inquiry and guide learning.

Key educator practices include:

- Planning around meaningful shared experiences
- Observing children's responses and interests
- Providing materials and prompts that extend learning
- Documenting and revisiting events through multiple media
- Connecting experiences to developmental goals

Benefits of Event-Based Learning

Real Life Relevance

Children learn in context. Events connect learning to real-life experiences, making it more meaningful and memorable.

Emotional Engagement

Events evoke feelings such as joy, curiosity and empathy that deepen engagement and support emotional development.

Narrative Thinking

Children make sense of events through stories. This supports language, memory, and reflective thinking.

Cultural Connection

Events honour family traditions, community practices, and seasonal rhythms. This fosters a sense of identity, belonging, and respect.

Integrated Learning

Events blend multiple domains, including literacy, numeracy, science, and art, into cohesive experiences.

Educator Responsiveness

Educators respond to teachable moments by planning intentionally, scaffolding instruction, and documenting progress. This ensures that learning is timely and purposeful.

Case Study: Arlo and the Market Visit

Arlo, age 5, visited a local farmers' market with his class. He was fascinated by the weighing scales and asked, "How do they know the price?" Back in the classroom, the educator set up a market stall with scales, play money, and produce. Children explored measurement, counting, and role-play by turning a simple outing into a rich, interdisciplinary project.

Learning Opportunities at Home

You can bring Event-Based Learning principles into your home by:

- Using family outings or celebrations as learning prompts
- Encouraging storytelling and reflection after shared experiences
- Offering materials to recreate or extend events through play
- Documenting your child's responses through photos or journals
- Connecting experiences to books, projects, or community resources

Thinking About Event-Based Learning

Ask yourself:

- Are children's experiences used as learning foundations?
- Is documentation visible and revisited?
- Are materials responsive to current events and interests?

Ask educators:

- "How do you plan learning around shared experiences?"
- "How do you document and extend children's responses?"
- "How do you connect events to developmental goals?"

Parent Pause

Reflect on:

- What recent experience sparked curiosity in your child?
- How do you support reflection and storytelling at home?
- What materials or routines help your child revisit meaningful events?

Event-based Based Learning transforms everyday experiences into powerful learning opportunities. It connects children to their world, their peers, and their own ideas. For families seeking relevance, responsiveness, and relational depth, this approach offers a joyful and grounded foundation.

Chapter 14: Emergent Curriculum

Following the Child's Lead

Emergent Curriculum is a child-centred approach that evolves from children's interests, questions, and interactions. Rather than following a fixed syllabus, educators observe, listen, and respond, designing learning experiences that reflect what matters most to the children in their care.

This model values flexibility, responsiveness, and co-construction. It treats curriculum as a living process, shaped by relationships, environments, and the unfolding discoveries of each day. For families, Emergent Curriculum offers a dynamic and deeply personalised path, one that honours the child's voice and the educator's insight.

An Emergent Curriculum learning environment is fluid, responsive, and alive with possibility. It's designed to reflect children's evolving interests, with materials, spaces, and documentation that adapt in real time.

Above all, an Emergent Curriculum environment is relational. It's built on trust, observation, and responsiveness. Educators and children co-create the curriculum together, shaping learning through shared experiences, questions, and reflections. It's a space where learning is meaningful, connected, and alive.

An emergent curriculum complements all other pedagogies:

- In play-based learning, educators observe and extend emerging themes.

- In inquiry-based learning, children's questions shape the direction of inquiry.
- In project-based learning, themes evolve through sustained investigation.
- In direct and explicit instruction, skills are taught in response to emerging needs.
- In intentional teaching, educators respond to teachable moments with purpose.
- In event-based learning, real-life experiences shape curriculum direction.

This integration ensures that learning is authentic, responsive, and deeply connected to children's lives.

The Role of the Educator

Educators in Emergent Curriculum settings are observers, co-learners, and responsive guides. They design curricula in real-time, based on children's interests and developmental needs.

Key educator practices include:

- Observing play and identifying emerging themes
- Planning flexible experiences that evolve with the child
- Asking open-ended questions to deepen inquiry
- Documenting learning and reflecting collaboratively

- Building strong, respectful relationships with children and families

Benefits of Emergent Curriculum

Child-Led Learning

Curriculum emerges from children's questions, play, and conversations. This affirms their agency and voice.

Deep Engagement

Children are more invested when learning reflects their interests. This leads to sustained attention and richer outcomes.

Flexibility and Responsiveness

Educators adapt plans based on observation and reflection. This ensures that learning is timely, relevant, and inclusive.

Creativity and Innovation

Emergent curriculum invites imagination. Children invent worlds, transform materials, and explore ideas in novel ways.

Relationship and Connection

The curriculum is co-constructed through dialogue and shared experiences. This strengthens relationships and builds community.

Documentation and Reflection

Educators document learning journeys, making thinking visible and guiding future planning. This supports professional growth and curriculum alignment.

Case Study: Mateo and the Broken Umbrella

Mateo, age 4, arrived at preschool on a rainy morning holding a broken umbrella. As he struggled to open it, he exclaimed, "It's not working! Why?" His educator paused, knelt beside him, and asked, "What do you think happened?" Mateo pointed to the bent spokes and said, "It's like a spider with a broken leg."

That moment sparked a class-wide inquiry. The educator documented Mateo's metaphor and invited the group to explore umbrellas, spiders, and mechanisms. Over the next two weeks, children:

- Investigated umbrella parts by disassembling old ones and comparing their structures
- Explored weather through rain journals, cloud watching, and water play
- Created spider webs using yarn, glue, and natural materials, inspired by Mateo's comparison
- Built prototypes of "better umbrellas" using recycled materials and tested them outdoors
- Wrote and illustrated stories about spider-umbrellas and rainy adventures
- Engaged in dramatic play, transforming the classroom into a weather station and repair shop

Throughout the inquiry, the educator introduced vocabulary such as "hinge," "fabric," "forecast," and "prototype," while documenting the children's theories and creations. Mateo's initial frustration became a catalyst for collaborative problem-solving, storytelling, and scientific exploration.

The inquiry concluded with a "Rainy Day Showcase," where children shared their umbrella designs and weather stories with families. Mateo proudly presented his "Spiderbrella", a taped-together invention with eight flexible arms and a waterproof shell.

Emergent Curriculum Principles at Home

You can bring Emergent Curriculum principles into your home by:

- Observing your child's play and interests
- Asking open-ended questions and following their lead
- Offering materials that support exploration and representation
- Documenting discoveries through photos, journals, or storytelling
- Creating flexible routines that allow for spontaneous learning

What to Look for in an Emergent Curriculum Program

Ask yourself:

- Is learning shaped by children's interests and questions?
- Is documentation visible and revisited?
- Are educators responsive and reflective?

Ask educators:

- "How do you plan curriculum based on observation?"
- "How do you document and extend children's inquiries?"
- "How do you balance flexibility with developmental goals?"

Parent Pause

Reflect on:

- What recent interest or question has your child expressed?
- How do you support spontaneous learning moments at home?
- What materials or routines help your child explore and express ideas?

Emergent Curriculum honours the child's voice and the educator's insight. It transforms everyday moments into meaningful learning and invites families to see curiosity as the heart of growth. For those seeking a responsive, relational, and inquiry-driven path, this approach offers depth, flexibility, and a sense of joy.

Part 3

Whole Child, Whole Community

Approaches that nurture emotional wellbeing, cultural identity, and holistic development—connecting learning to life

In Part 3, we explore approaches that honour the whole child not just as a learner, but as a feeling, thinking, growing human being. These chapters invite families to reflect on emotional wellbeing, cultural identity, autonomy, and the powerful role of relationships and community in early learning.

Children thrive when they are seen, heard, and supported in every dimension of their development. That means nurturing not only their cognitive growth, but their emotional safety, sense of belonging, and connection to the world around them. It means choosing environments that reflect your family's values, honour your child's identity, and build bridges between home, school, and community.

This section includes approaches that centre empathy, curiosity, attachment, nature, and cultural competence. It also explores how educators blend philosophies with purpose, and how families can make informed choices that align with their child's needs and strengths.

Above all, Part 3 reinforces a fundamental truth: learning is a relational process. When children feel safe, valued, and connected, they flourish not only academically but also socially, emotionally, and spiritually. By embracing a whole-child, whole-community lens, we create learning environments that are not only effective but also compassionate, inclusive, and enduring.

Chapter 15: Holistic Approach

Whole Child Development

The Holistic Approach views children as whole beings, encompassing their intellectual, emotional, physical, social, and spiritual aspects. It emphasises balance across developmental domains, recognising that learning is deeply connected to wellbeing, relationships, creativity, and identity. Educators using this approach design experiences that nurture the whole child, integrating movement, mindfulness, emotional safety, and real-world relevance.

Rather than focusing solely on academic outcomes, holistic education supports children in becoming confident, compassionate, and self-aware individuals. It's a model that values presence, connection, and growth in every dimension.

Why It Matters

- Whole-child development predicts lifelong wellbeing. Emotional regulation, social skills, and physical health in early childhood are linked to better outcomes in education, relationships, and mental health.

- Children learn best when they feel safe and connected. Neuroscience shows that secure relationships and emotional safety activate the brain's capacity for learning.

- Integrated experiences reflect how children naturally think. Young children don't compartmentalise subjects, they learn through play, story, movement, and inquiry.

- Creativity and movement support executive function. Research highlights the role of expressive arts and physical activity in building memory, attention, and problem-solving skills.

- Spiritual and ethical development begins early. A child's sense of wonder, purpose, and belonging are vital aspects of growth, often nurtured through holistic practices.

Case Study: Amira and the Peace Garden

Amira, age 5, often felt overwhelmed in busy environments. Her educator created a "peace garden" corner with soft cushions, calming scents, and nature objects. Amira began visiting the space daily, drawing, breathing, and reflecting. Over time, she invited peers to join her, creating rituals of care and connection. The peace garden became a shared sanctuary, supporting emotional regulation, creativity, and friendship.

Holistic Approaches at Home

You can bring holistic principles into your home by:

- Creating calming spaces for reflection and creativity

- Integrating movement, nature, and mindfulness into daily routines

- Valuing emotional expression and open dialogue
- Offering materials that support exploration and self-awareness
- Celebrating growth in all areas, not just academic

What to Look for in a Holistic Program

Ask yourself:

- Is the environment calm, beautiful, and emotionally safe?
- Are children's inner lives and outer experiences honoured?
- Is creativity, movement, and nature integrated?

Ask educators:

- "How do you support the whole child's development?"
- "How do you integrate emotional wellbeing into learning?"
- "How do you create space for reflection and connection?"

Parent Pause

Reflect on:

- What helps your child feel calm, connected, and curious?
- How do you support emotional and creative expression at home?
- What routines or values nurture your child's whole development?

The Holistic Approach reminds us that children are more than learners, they are whole beings. By supporting their emotional, physical, creative, and spiritual growth, we create environments that enable them to thrive in every dimension. For families seeking depth, balance, and authenticity, this approach offers a nurturing and expansive foundation.

Chapter 16: Cultural Competence

Learning Through Identity

Cultural competence in early childhood education involves recognising, respecting, and responding to the diverse identities of children, their families, and the communities in which they live. It's not just about celebrating difference; it's about embedding equity, belonging, and representation into every aspect of learning.

Educators practising cultural competence actively reflect on their own biases, build inclusive environments, and co-create curriculum that honours children's languages, histories, and lived experiences. This approach helps children feel seen, valued, and empowered to express themselves authentically.

Why It Matters

- Identity is foundational to wellbeing. When children feel proud of who they are, they develop confidence, resilience, and a strong sense of belonging.

- Early experiences shape lifelong attitudes. Exposure to inclusive environments helps children build empathy, challenge stereotypes, and embrace diversity.

- Representation matters. Seeing their culture reflected in books, materials, and educators' language affirms children's worth and strengthens family-school partnerships.

- Cultural competence supports equity. It helps educators recognise systemic barriers and create learning spaces that are fair, responsive, and inclusive.

- Language and culture are learning tools. Children learn best when their home languages and cultural practices are integrated into the curriculum.

Case Study: Zain and the Ramadan Table

Zain, age 4, was excited to share that his family was preparing for Ramadan. His educator invited him to help create a "Ramadan Table" in the classroom, filled with books, photos, and objects from home. Zain explained fasting, family traditions, and nighttime prayers to his peers. The table became a hub for storytelling, art, and reflection. Children asked questions, made lanterns, and learned about empathy and the celebration of diversity. Zain beamed with pride, and his classmates gained a deeper understanding of cultural diversity.

Cultural Competence at Home

You can support cultural competence at home by:

- Sharing stories, songs, and traditions from your family's background

- Reading books that reflect diverse cultures, languages, and identities

- Encouraging your child to ask questions and celebrate differences

- Connecting with educators to share your child's cultural strengths
- Reflecting on your own cultural lens and how it shapes parenting

What to Look for in a Culturally Competent Program

Ask yourself:

- Is diversity visible in books, materials, and displays?
- Are children's languages and traditions honoured?
- Is inclusion embedded, not just celebrated occasionally?

Ask educators:

- "How do you support cultural identity in your program?"
- "How do you build relationships with families from diverse backgrounds?"
- "How do you reflect on your own cultural lens and bias?"

Parent Pause

Reflect on:

- What cultural traditions or values are important in your family?
- How does your child express their identity?
- What helps your child feel proud, safe, and included?

Cultural competence is about more than diversity; it's about dignity, belonging, and justice. When children see their identity reflected and respected, they flourish. For families seeking inclusive and empowering environments, this approach offers a foundation rooted in respect, relationships, and representation.

Chapter 17: Respectful Approach

Empathy and Autonomy

The Respectful Approach centres on the belief that children deserve the same dignity, empathy, and autonomy as adults. It's grounded in relational care where educators listen deeply, respond gently, and support children's agency without coercion or control.

This model draws on philosophies such as Magda Gerber's RIE (Resources for Infant Educarers), the Pikler approach, and trauma-informed practice. It emphasises attuned caregiving, clear boundaries, and emotional safety. Respectful educators see behaviour as communication and respond with curiosity, not correction.

Why It Matters

- Secure relationships build resilience. Neuroscience reveals that attuned, respectful interactions foster brain development and enhance emotional regulation.

- Empathy fosters self-worth. When children are treated with kindness and understanding, they internalise those qualities and extend them to others.

- Autonomy supports motivation. Children who are given choices and trusted to lead their own learning develop confidence, initiative, and problem-solving skills.

- Respectful care reduces power struggles. By honouring the child's perspective, educators create cooperative, emotionally safe environments.

- Emotional literacy begins with modelling. Children learn empathy, boundaries, and self-regulation through the way adults speak, listen, and respond.

Case Study: Eli and the Shoe Dilemma

Eli, age 3, became upset when asked to put on his shoes before going outside for play. Instead of insisting, his educator knelt beside him and said, "You're not ready yet. I wonder what's bothering you." Eli pointed to the tight strap and said, "It hurts." The educator offered a different pair and gave Eli time to make a choice. Within minutes, he was outside, smiling and engaged. By responding with empathy and offering autonomy, the educator turned a potential power struggle into a moment of trust and connection.

Respect at Home

You can support respectful practice at home by:

- Narrating routines with empathy ("I'm going to pick you up now so we can get ready")

- Offering choices within boundaries ("Would you like the red cup or the blue one?")

- Listening without rushing to fix or correct

- Validating emotions before redirecting behaviour
- Modelling respectful language and tone even during conflict

What to Look for in a Respectful Program

Ask yourself:

- Are children spoken to with warmth and clarity?
- Are routines predictable, gentle, and attuned to the child's pace?
- Is autonomy supported through choice and trust?

Ask educators:

- "How do you respond to children's emotions and behaviour?"
- "How do you support autonomy and agency?"
- "How do you build respectful relationships with families?"

Parent Pause

Reflect on:

- How do you respond when your child resists a routine or boundary?
- What helps you stay calm and connected during challenging moments?
- How do you model empathy and respect in your daily interactions?

A Respectful Approach reminds us that children are not just small learners; they are whole human beings. When we meet them with empathy and honour their autonomy, we build relationships rooted in trust, dignity, and emotional safety. For families seeking connection over control, this approach offers a path of deep respect and lasting resilience.

Chapter 18: Curiosity Approach

Awe and Wonder

The Curiosity Approach is a modern educational philosophy that encourages children to explore the world with awe, wonder, and open-ended inquiry. It blends elements from Reggio Emilia, Steiner, Montessori, and Te Whāriki, but its heart lies in creating environments that spark fascination and invite deep thinking.

Educators using this approach prioritise natural materials, sensory experiences, and provocations that stimulate curiosity and foster a love of learning. Rather than directing learning, they observe, listen, and co-explore, trusting that children's questions, theories, and discoveries will lead to meaningful growth.

Why It Matters

- Curiosity drives learning. Neuroscience shows that when children are curious, their brains are primed for deeper engagement and retention.

- Wonder fosters emotional connection. Experiences that evoke awe, such as watching a butterfly emerge or hearing a story unfold, build empathy, joy, and reflection.

- Open-ended exploration supports creativity. Children learn to think flexibly, solve problems, and express themselves in a variety of ways.

- Slow, intentional learning builds resilience. The Curiosity Approach values process over product, helping children develop patience, focus, and self-regulation.

- Natural environments support wellbeing. Exposure to beauty, texture, and nature reduces stress and enhances sensory integration.

Case Study: Alex and the Shadow Wall

Alex, age 4, noticed his shadow stretching across the floor and asked, "Why is it longer now?" His educator paused, then invited Alex to explore. Over the next week, the class created a "Shadow Wall" using torches, tracing paper, and natural objects. They experimented with light, movement, and storytelling, drawing shadow creatures and mapping sun patterns. Alex's question led to a rich inquiry that blended science, art, and wonder.

Home Applications

You can nurture curiosity at home by:

- Slowing down and noticing beauty in everyday moments
- Asking open-ended questions ("What do you think will happen next?")
- Offering natural materials for play and exploration
- Creating quiet spaces for observation, reflection, and storytelling

- Valuing your child's questions even when you don't have the answers

What to Look for in an Early Childhood Program

Ask yourself:

- Is the environment calm, beautiful, and filled with natural materials?
- Are children's questions and theories visible in documentation?
- Is learning paced intentionally, with room for wonder?

Ask educators:

- "How do you foster curiosity and inquiry?"
- "How do you respond to children's questions and ideas?"
- "How do you balance structure with open-ended exploration?"

Parent Pause

Reflect on:

- What sparks wonder in your child?
- How do you respond when they ask significant or unexpected questions?
- What helps you slow down and see the world through their eyes?

Fostering curiosity encourages children to develop a passion for learning. It honours their questions, celebrates their discoveries, and creates space for awe. For families who value beauty, reflection, and deep engagement, this approach provides a gentle yet powerful path to whole-child development.

Chapter 19: Attachment-Based Approach

Relationships First

The Attachment-Based Approach centres on the idea that secure relationships are the foundation of all learning. It draws from attachment theory, which emphasises the importance of consistent, responsive caregiving in helping children feel safe, regulated, and ready to explore.

In early childhood settings, this approach means educators prioritise connection before correction. They build trust through attuned interactions, predictable routines, and emotional availability. Children are not managed, they are understood. Their behaviour is seen as communication, and their emotional needs are met with empathy and presence.

Why It Matters

- Secure attachment supports brain development. Neuroscience reveals that consistent, loving relationships foster the development of neural pathways that support emotional regulation, attention, and resilience.

- Children thrive when they feel safe. A secure base allows children to explore, take risks, and engage deeply with learning.

- Behaviour is relational. Challenging behaviours often stem from unmet emotional needs. Attachment-informed educators respond with curiosity, not punishment.

- Relationships buffer stress. In times of transition, trauma, or uncertainty, strong relationships help children feel anchored and supported.

- Connection builds confidence. When children know they are loved and understood, they develop a strong sense of self and trust in others.

Case Study: Charlie and the Morning Drop-Off

Charlie, age 3, struggled with separation at morning drop-off. His educator noticed that Charlie clung to his mother and cried intensely. Instead of rushing the transition, she created a "connection ritual", a special greeting song, a photo of Charlie's family in his cubby, and a consistent caregiver to welcome him each day. Over time, Charlie began to anticipate the ritual, and his tears lessened. He formed a strong bond with his educator, and his confidence grew. The relationship became his bridge to learning.

At Home

You can support attachment-based principles at home by:

- Creating predictable routines that help your child feel safe
- Responding to emotions with empathy before offering solutions
- Using rituals to ease transitions (e.g., goodbye songs, special handshakes)

- Staying present during moments of distress, even when you don't have answers
- Building connection through play, storytelling, and shared attention

What to Look for in a Program that Supports Attachment Theory

Ask yourself:

- Are relationships prioritised over routines and outcomes?
- Do educators respond to behaviour with empathy and curiosity?
- Is emotional safety visible in the way children are greeted, comforted, and supported?

Ask educators:

- "How do you build secure relationships with children?"
- "How do you support children during emotional or behavioural challenges?"
- "How do you help families feel connected to the learning environment?"

Parent Pause

Reflect on:

- What helps your child feel safe and connected during transitions?

- How do you respond when your child is overwhelmed or dysregulated?
- What rituals or routines strengthen your bond with your child?

Being mindful of attachment theory reminds us that relationships are not just important, they are everything. When children feel safe, seen, and soothed, they are free to learn, grow, and thrive. For families seeking emotional depth and relational care, this approach offers a robust foundation rooted in love, trust, and connection.

Chapter 20: Nature Pedagogy

Learning Through the Land

Nature Pedagogy is an educational philosophy that places the natural world at the heart of children's learning. It's more than just outdoor play; it's a way of being that recognises the land as teacher, the environment as co-educator, and nature as a source of wisdom, wonder, and wellbeing.

Educators practising nature pedagogy create opportunities for children to explore, observe, and connect with the living world. They embrace seasonal rhythms, Indigenous perspectives, and ecological responsibility. Learning is slow, sensory, and rooted in place. Children are encouraged to build relationships with the land, rather than just using it.

Why It Matters

- Nature supports whole-child development. Outdoor environments promote physical health, emotional regulation, creativity, and resilience.

- Connection to land fosters belonging. When children build relationships with place, they develop a sense of stewardship and identity.

- Sensory experiences deepen learning. Touching bark, smelling the rain, and hearing birdsong engage the body and mind in an integrated way.

- Risk and challenge build confidence. Climbing, balancing, and navigating uneven terrain help children develop strength, coordination, and problem-solving skills.

- Nature invites reflection and awe. Quiet moments in natural settings support emotional wellbeing and spiritual growth.

Case Study: Tilly and the Rain Tree

Tilly, age 4, noticed that a tree in the outdoor space looked different after a storm. "It's crying," she said, pointing to the dripping leaves. Her educator invited the group to observe the tree over several days by tracking changes, collecting fallen leaves, and drawing what they saw. The inquiry led to conversations about weather, water cycles, and tree emotions. Tilly's poetic observation became a touchstone for empathy, science, and storytelling, all of which were rooted in her relationship with the land.

Nature-Based Approaches at Home

You can bring nature pedagogy into your home by:

- Spending time outdoors in all weather: walking, sitting, noticing

- Encouraging your child to observe seasonal changes and natural patterns

- Creating rituals around nature (e.g., morning sun greetings, rain dances, moon stories)

- Using natural materials for play, such as sticks, stones, leaves, and water
- Talking about land with respect, curiosity, and gratitude

What to Look for in a Nature-Based Program

Ask yourself:

- Is nature integrated into daily routines, not just scheduled as "outdoor time"?
- Are children encouraged to explore, take risks, and build relationships with place?
- Is the environment wild, diverse, and responsive, not overly manicured?

Ask educators:

- "How do you use nature as a teacher?"
- "How do you support children's connection to land and place?"
- "How do you incorporate Indigenous perspectives or ecological responsibility?"

Parent Pause

Reflect on:

- What natural places feel meaningful to your child or to you?
- How does your child respond to being outdoors?

- What helps your family slow down and connect with the living world?

Nature Pedagogy invites children to learn through relationships with the land, with the seasons, and with themselves. It's a gentle, powerful approach that nurtures curiosity, resilience, and reverence. For families seeking depth, connection, and ecological awareness, this model offers a path rooted in wonder and belonging.

Chapter 21: Play Schema Theory

Understanding Patterns in Play

Play Schema Theory is a lens for understanding how children explore the world through repeated, patterned behaviours. These schemas, such as transporting, enveloping, rotating, or connecting, are not random; they're expressions of deep cognitive processing and developmental growth.

Educators who recognise play schemas observe children closely, identify their dominant patterns, and offer materials and experiences that extend those interests. Rather than interrupting or redirecting repetitive play, they see it as purposeful, intelligent, and worthy of support.

Why It Matters

- Schemas reveal how children think. Repetitive play behaviours are signs of internal learning processes, helping children test theories and build understanding.

- Supporting schemas boosts engagement. When educators respond to a child's schema, they validate their curiosity and deepen their focus.

- Schemas connect to developmental milestones. Many schemas align with emerging skills in motor coordination, spatial awareness, and symbolic thinking.

- Understanding schemas reduces misinterpretation. Behaviours like dumping, wrapping, or spinning may seem disruptive, but through a schema lens, they're meaningful and developmental.
- Schema-informed practice builds trust. Children feel seen and supported when adults understand the "why" behind their play.

Types of Play

Type of Play	Developmental Age Range	Description	Example	Common Schema Links
Unoccupied Play	Birth–3 months	Random movements and sensory exploration without a clear purpose.	A newborn waves arms and legs while gazing at light.	None yet — early sensory regulation
Solitary Play	0–2 years	Playing alone, focused on own activity, unaware of others nearby.	A toddler stacks blocks quietly in a corner.	Enclosing, trajectory, rotation
Onlooker Play	2–3 years	Watching others play without joining in; learning through observation.	A child watches peers build a sandcastle but doesn't participate.	Developing interest in positioning, connection
Parallel Play	2–3.5 years	Playing side-by-side with similar materials but without interaction.	Two children draw with crayons at the same table; each focused on their own page.	Transporting, enveloping, trajectory
Associative Play	3–4.5 years	Playing near others with some interaction, but no shared goals or rules.	Children share toy cars and chat while driving them around.	Rotation, connecting, enveloping
Cooperative Play	4–6+ years	Playing with shared goals, rules, and roles; requires	A group of children build a fort together, assigning roles	Connecting, orientation, positioning

			communication and teamwork.	like "builder" and "guard."	
Symbolic (Pretend) Play	2.5–7 years		Using imagination to represent objects, roles, or scenarios.	A child uses a banana as a phone and pretends to call grandma.	Enveloping, transforming, trajectory
Constructive Play	2–6 years		Creating or building something with materials; goal-oriented.	A child builds a tower with blocks or makes a collage with recycled items.	Connecting, enclosing, positioning
Physical (Motor) Play	0–6+ years		Using the body to explore movement, strength, and coordination.	A toddler climbs a soft structure; a preschooler plays tag.	Trajectory, rotation, orientation
Sensory Play	6 months–6+ years		Exploring textures, sounds, smells, and other senses.	A child squishes playdough, pours water, or digs in sand.	Enveloping, trajectory, transformation
Rough-and-Tumble Play	3–7+ years		Energetic, physical play with peers; often includes play fighting or chasing.	Children wrestle gently or play "monster chase" with laughter and boundaries.	Trajectory, orientation, rotation
Exploratory Play	6 months–3 years		Investigating objects and environments to understand how things work.	A baby drops a spoon repeatedly to see what happens; a toddler opens and closes containers.	Containment, trajectory, rotation
Role Play / Socio-Dramatic Play	3–7+ years		Acting out real-life roles and scenarios with others.	Children pretend to run a café, take orders, and serve food.	Enveloping, transforming, connecting
Games with Rules	5–8+ years		Structured play with agreed-upon rules and turn-taking.	Children play "Duck Duck Goose" or board games	Positioning, orientation, connecting

			like "Snakes and Ladders."	

Reflection

Take a moment to observe your child's play this week. Use the prompts below to deepen your understanding and connection:

- What types of play does your child return to most often?
- Do you notice any repeated patterns, such as transporting, wrapping, spinning, or lining up?
- How do you respond when play feels repetitive, messy, or intense?
- What materials or environments seem to support your child's preferred play style?
- How might you extend their play by offering new tools, space, or language?

Case Study: Arlo and the Transporting Schema

Arlo, age 3, spent hours moving objects from one place to another. He placed blocks in buckets, cars in baskets, and even sand in his pockets. His educator recognised a strong transporting schema and responded by offering wheelbarrows, baskets, and tubes. Arlo's play expanded into building delivery systems, mapping routes, and storytelling. What once looked like repetitive behaviour became a rich inquiry into movement, purpose, and design.

Play Schemas at Home

You can support play schemas at home by:

- Observing your child's repeated behaviours, what patterns do you notice?
- Offering materials that match their schema (e.g., containers for transporting, fabric for enveloping)
- Creating safe spaces for schema play, even if it's messy or unconventional
- Narrating their actions with curiosity ("You're wrapping everything today, what's your plan?")
- Valuing repetition as a sign of deep learning, not something to "fix"

What to Look for in a Schema-Informed Program

Ask yourself:

- Are educators observing and documenting children's play patterns?
- Are materials and environments responsive to children's schemas?
- Is repetition seen as meaningful, not problematic?

Ask educators:

- "How do you identify and support play schemas?"
- "Can you tell me what schemas my child is exploring?"

- "How do you extend learning based on those patterns?"

Parent Pause

Reflect on:

- What play patterns does your child return to again and again?
- How do you respond when play feels repetitive or intense?
- What helps you see your child's behaviour through a lens of curiosity?

Play Schema Theory invites us to look beneath the surface of children's behaviour and see the brilliance within. When we understand the patterns they're exploring, we can support learning that's deep, joyful, and truly child-led. For families seeking insight into their child's inner world, this approach offers a powerful key.

Chapter 22: Integrated Approaches

Blending Philosophies with Purpose

Integrated Approaches combine elements from multiple educational philosophies to create a flexible, responsive model tailored to the needs of children, families, and communities. Rather than adhering strictly to one framework, educators draw from diverse traditions, including Montessori, Reggio Emilia, Steiner, and inquiry-based learning, among others, blending practices that align with their values and context.

This approach is intentional, not eclectic. It requires a deep understanding of each philosophy's principles and a clear rationale for how they're combined. Integrated educators continually reflect on their practice, adapting it to support whole-child development while honouring cultural, relational, and environmental factors.

Why It Matters

- Children are diverse so learning should be too. No single philosophy fits every child, family, or community. Integrated approaches offer flexibility and responsiveness.

- Blending models supports holistic development. Educators can draw on the strengths of each philosophy. For example, Montessori's emphasis on independence, Reggio's focus on creativity, and Steiner's emphasis on rhythm to meet the varied developmental needs of their students.

- Integration encourages innovation. Educators become co-designers of learning, crafting environments and experiences that evolve with children's interests and growth.

- Families benefit from transparency. When educators explain why they've chosen certain practices, families feel informed, empowered, and included.

- Purposeful integration avoids confusion. Without clear intention, blending philosophies can feel scattered. Integrated approaches require coherence, reflection, and shared language.

Case Study: The River Room

In a mixed-age preschool called the River Room, educators noticed that children were drawn to both structured tasks and open-ended exploration. They blended Montessori principles (individual work trays and practical life activities) with Reggio-inspired provocations (natural materials and collaborative art) and Steiner rhythms (seasonal songs and storytelling). One week, children harvested herbs from the garden, prepared tea using Montessori tools, and created nature journals with watercolour illustrations. The educators documented the process, linking it to developmental goals and family values. The result was a rich, integrated experience that honoured autonomy, creativity, and connection.

Integrated Learning at Home

You can support integrated learning at home by:

- Exploring multiple educational philosophies and noticing what resonates with your child
- Creating a blend of structure and freedom, like routines, with room for creativity
- Offering materials that support independence (e.g., child-sized tools) and imagination (e.g., loose parts, art supplies)
- Reflecting on your family's values and how they shape your parenting choices
- Asking educators about the "why" behind their practices and sharing your own insights

What to Look for in an Integrated Program

Ask yourself:

- Is there clarity and intention behind the blend of philosophies?
- Are children's needs, interests, and identities guiding the integration?
- Is the environment coherent, responsive, and inclusive?

Ask educators:

- "What philosophies influence your practice, and how do you blend them?"
- "How do you ensure consistency and clarity across your approach?"

- "How do you involve families in shaping the learning environment?"

Parent Pause

Reflect on:

- What educational values matter most to your family?
- How do you balance structure and freedom in your home?
- What helps you feel confident when choosing a learning environment for your child?

Integrated Approaches remind us that education is not one-size-fits-all. When philosophies are blended with purpose, children benefit from rich, responsive learning that honours their individuality and supports their growth. For families seeking flexibility, depth, and clarity, this approach offers a thoughtful path forward.

Chapter 23: Eclectic Approach

Responsive and Adaptive Practice

The Eclectic Approach is a flexible and adaptive model that draws from multiple educational philosophies without rigid allegiance to any one of them. Unlike integrated approaches, which blend frameworks with clear structure, eclectic practice is more fluid, responding to the child, the moment, and the context with whatever tools best support learning.

Educators using this approach are reflective and resourceful. They may shift between Montessori independence, Reggio-inspired inquiry, Steiner rhythm, or play-based spontaneity, depending on the needs of the group or individual child. The key is responsiveness: choosing what works, when it works, for whom it works.

Why It Matters

- Children's needs change daily. Eclectic educators can pivot quickly, offering support that's developmentally appropriate and emotionally attuned.

- Flexibility supports inclusion. Diverse learners, especially neurodivergent children or those with trauma backgrounds, benefit from adaptable environments.

- No single philosophy fits every moment. Eclectic practice allows educators to respond to real-life complexity with creativity and care.

- Families feel seen. When educators adapt to cultural values, parenting styles, and individual preferences, families feel respected and included.

- Reflection drives growth. Eclectic educators must constantly evaluate their choices, ensuring that flexibility doesn't become inconsistency.

Case Study: Noor and the Quiet Corner

Noor, age 4, was sensitive to noise and transitions. Her educator noticed that structured group activities often overwhelmed her. Drawing from Steiner's rhythm, they created a predictable daily flow. From Montessori, they offered independent work trays. From Reggio, they added a quiet corner with natural materials and soft light. Noor began choosing the quiet corner during transitions, regulating herself and rejoining the group when ready. The educator's eclectic response honoured Noor's needs without forcing conformity.

Eclectic Principles at Home

You can support eclectic principles at home by:

- Trusting your instincts and responding to your child's needs rather than following rigid rules

- Blending structure and spontaneity based on your child's temperament

- Drawing from multiple parenting philosophies and adapting them to your family's values

- Creating flexible spaces and routines that allow for choice, rest, and creativity

- Reflecting regularly on what's working and what needs to shift

What to Look for in an Eclectic Program

Ask yourself:

- Is the environment adaptable and responsive, not overly rigid or chaotic?

- Are educators attuned to individual needs and willing to shift their approach?

- Is there evidence of reflection and intentionality behind the flexibility?

Ask educators:

- "How do you adapt your practice to meet individual children's needs?"

- "What philosophies influence your work, and how do you decide what to use?"

- "How do you ensure consistency while remaining flexible?"

Parent Pause

Reflect on:

- What helps your child feel safe, engaged, and understood?

- How do you adapt your parenting when your child's needs shift?
- What philosophies or practices have you blended in your own approach?

The Eclectic Approach reminds us that responsiveness is a strength. When educators and families adapt with intention, children receive what they need when they need it. For those seeking flexibility without sacrificing depth, this model provides a compassionate and creative path forward.

Chapter 24: Choosing What's Right for Your Family

This chapter isn't about a single philosophy; it's about the process of choosing. With so many early childhood education approaches available, families often feel overwhelmed or uncertain. Choosing what's right for your child means understanding your values, your child's temperament, and the kind of learning environment that feels safe, inspiring, and aligned.

This is a reflective, relational process. It's not about finding the "best" approach; it's about finding the one that fits. Families are encouraged to explore, ask questions, and trust their instincts. The goal is not perfection, but connection.

Why It Matters

- Every child is unique. What works beautifully for one child may not work as well for another. Responsive choices honour individuality.

- Family values shape learning. Education is not separate from parenting; it's an extension of your beliefs, hopes, and culture.

- Confidence supports advocacy. When families understand their priorities, they can ask informed questions and advocate for their child's needs.

- There's no single "right" answer, just thoughtful decisions made with love and intention.

- Partnership builds trust. When families and educators collaborate, children benefit from consistency and mutual respect.

You can support thoughtful decision-making by:

- Reflecting on your child's temperament, interests, and emotional needs
- Discussing your family's values around learning, discipline, creativity, and community
- Visiting programs and observing how your child responds to the environment
- Asking educators about their philosophy and how they adapt to individual children
- Trusting your instincts even if your choice looks different from others'

What to Look for When Choosing a Program

Ask yourself:

- Does this environment feel emotionally safe and welcoming?
- Can I see my child thriving here, not just surviving?
- Do the educators speak with warmth, clarity, and respect?
- What matters most to you in your child's early learning experience?

- How does your child respond to structure, freedom, creativity, or routine?
- What helps you feel confident and connected when making decisions?

Additional questions for educators:

- "How do you adapt your approach to meet individual children's needs?"
- "What role do families play in your program?"
- "How do you support emotional wellbeing, creativity, and autonomy?"

Case Study: The Martins' Journey

The Martin family had three children with very different personalities. Their eldest thrived in a Montessori setting, independent and focused. Their middle child, a sensitive and imaginative individual, found joy in a Reggio-inspired preschool. Their youngest, most energetic, and social child flourished in a play-based cooperative. The Martins didn't choose one philosophy; they decided what fit each child. They visited programs, asked questions, and reflected together. Their journey was guided not by trends, but by trust.

Choosing an early childhood approach is not a test; it's a relationship. When families reflect, explore, and trust their instincts, they create a foundation of safety, joy, and growth. For those seeking clarity in a complex landscape, this chapter offers permission to choose with heart, not just with logic.

Decision-Making Worksheet

Choosing an Early Childhood Approach That Fits Your Family

✦ Step 1: Know Your Child

What are your child's strengths, interests, and sensitivities?

☐ Enjoys structure and routine

☐ Thrives in open-ended, creative play

☐ Needs emotional support during transitions

☐ Loves movement and outdoor exploration

☐ Prefers quiet, focused activities

☐ Seeks social connection and teamwork

☐ Other: _____

What helps your child feel safe, confident, and curious?

_____

_____

_____

✦ Step 2: Know Your Family

Which values matter most in your child's early learning?

☐ Independence and self-direction

☐ Emotional wellbeing and empathy

☐ Creativity and imagination

☐ Cultural identity and inclusion

☐ Academic readiness and structure

- ☐ Nature connection and sustainability
- ☐ Flexibility and responsiveness
- ☐ Other: _____

What kind of relationship do you want with your child's educators?
- ☐ Collaborative and communicative
- ☐ Trust-based with shared values
- ☐ Flexible and open to feedback
- ☐ Other: _____

✦ Step 3: Explore the Environment

When visiting a program, ask yourself:
- ☐ Does the space feel emotionally safe and welcoming?
- ☐ Are children engaged, joyful, and respected?
- ☐ Is the philosophy visible in daily routines and materials?
- ☐ Are educators warm, attuned, and reflective?
- ☐ Is documentation used to make learning visible?
- ☐ Can I imagine my child thriving here?

✦ Step 4: Ask Educators

Helpful questions to guide your conversation:

- "What philosophies influence your practice?"
- "How do you adapt your approach to meet individual children's needs?"

- "How do you support emotional wellbeing and autonomy?"
- "How do you involve families in the learning journey?"
- "Can you share a recent example of child-led learning?"

- _____
- _____
- _____
- _____

✦ Step 5: Reflect and Decide

What feels aligned with your child's needs and your family's values?

_____

_____

What questions or concerns do you still have?

_____

_____

What's your next step?

☐ Schedule a visit

☐ Talk with your child

☐ Reflect as a family

☐ Trust your instincts

☐ Other: _____

_____

"There's no perfect choice—only a thoughtful one. When you choose with love, clarity, and trust, your child will feel it."

Chapter 25: Foundations for Life

Throughout this guide, you've explored the rich landscape of early childhood education, from play schemas and nature pedagogy to inquiry-based learning and integrated approaches. Each chapter has offered a lens, a language, and a set of tools to help you see your child's education with clarity, compassion, and confidence.

But more than anything, this book has been about the relationships between children and caregivers, families and educators, and the questions and discoveries that arise from them. It's about building foundations that last a lifetime.

What You Now Hold

- Clarity about the diverse approaches available and how they align with your child's needs

- Confidence to ask questions, observe environments, and trust your instincts

- Language to describe your values, advocate for your child, and engage with educators

- Reflection on your parenting journey, your child's unique path, and your hopes for their future

- Connection to a community of families who are choosing with intention, not just convention

What Comes Next

There is no final answer, only ongoing discovery. As your child grows, so will your questions, your insights, and your choices. You may revisit this guide, shift your approach, or find new meaning in familiar ideas. That's not inconsistency, it's growth.

Whether you choose Montessori or Reggio, play-based or inquiry-led, what matters most is that your choice is rooted in love, reflection, and responsiveness.

Take a moment to honour your journey:

- What have you learned about your child and yourself through this process?
- What values will guide your decisions moving forward?
- What kind of learning environment feels like home for your family?

Final Thoughts

You are your child's first teacher, fiercest advocate, and most trusted guide. This book is not the end; it's a beginning. A foundation. A companion as you walk alongside your child with curiosity, courage, and care.

Thank you for choosing to learn, reflect, and lead with heart. The future you're building is bright, and it begins right here.

About the Author

Ariston Kace is a community-focused educator, teacher, author, and program coordinator specialising in early childhood education. With over a decade of experience supporting families, educators, and children, Ariston brings clarity, warmth, and evidence-based insight to every resource she creates.

Her work is grounded in empathy and emotional intelligence, blending developmental theory with real-world application.

Ariston's writing is inspired by her three children, who remain her greatest teachers. Their questions, play, and perspectives are woven throughout this guide, honouring the everyday wisdom of childhood.

www.ingramcontent.com/pod-product-compliance
Lightning Source LLC
Chambersburg PA
CBHW061208070526
44583CB00025B/3168